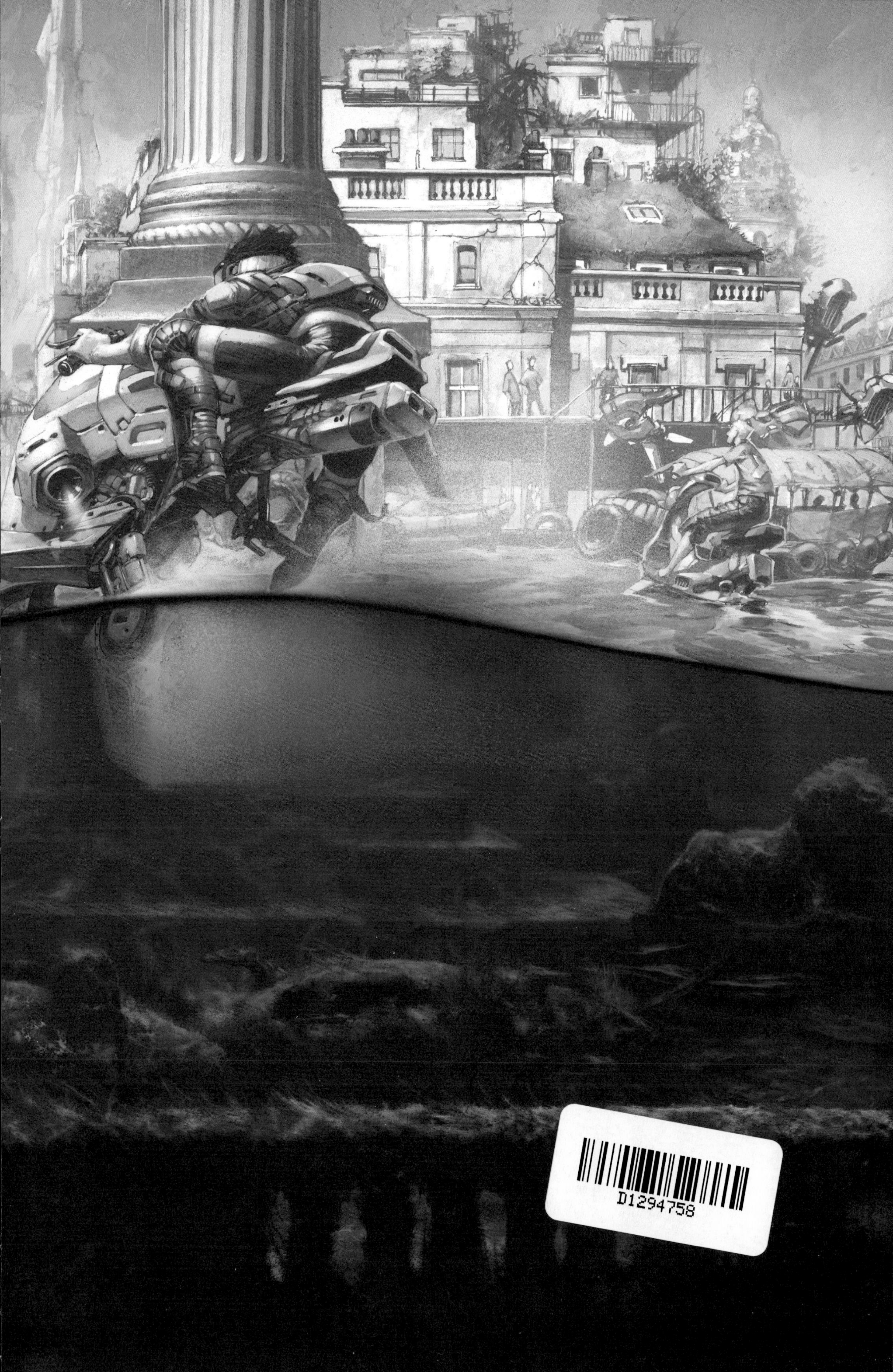

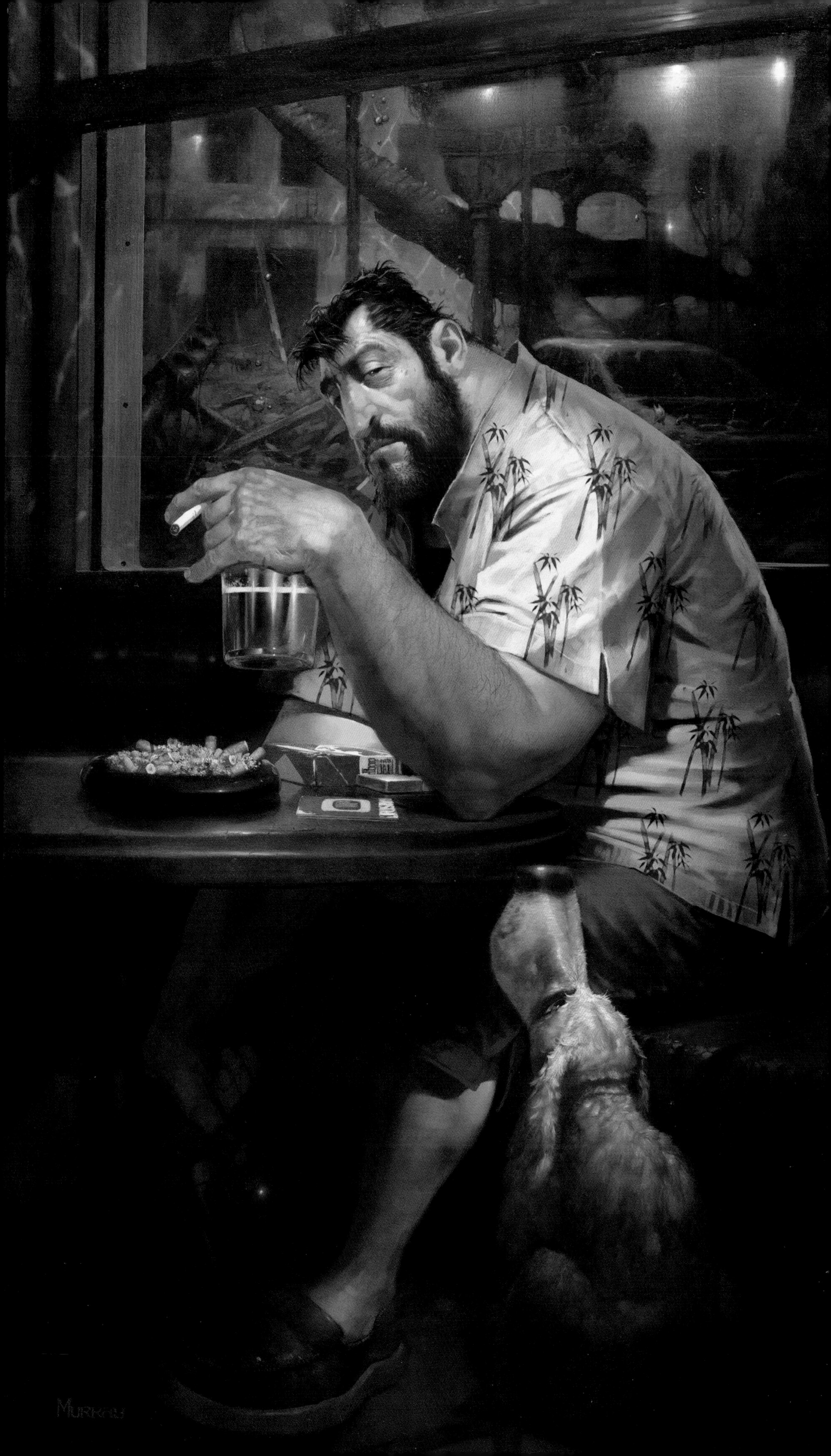

To Deborah

For the title and so many other reasons
that they'd need a book to themselves.


To Annabel

# DROWNTOWN

## BOOK ONE



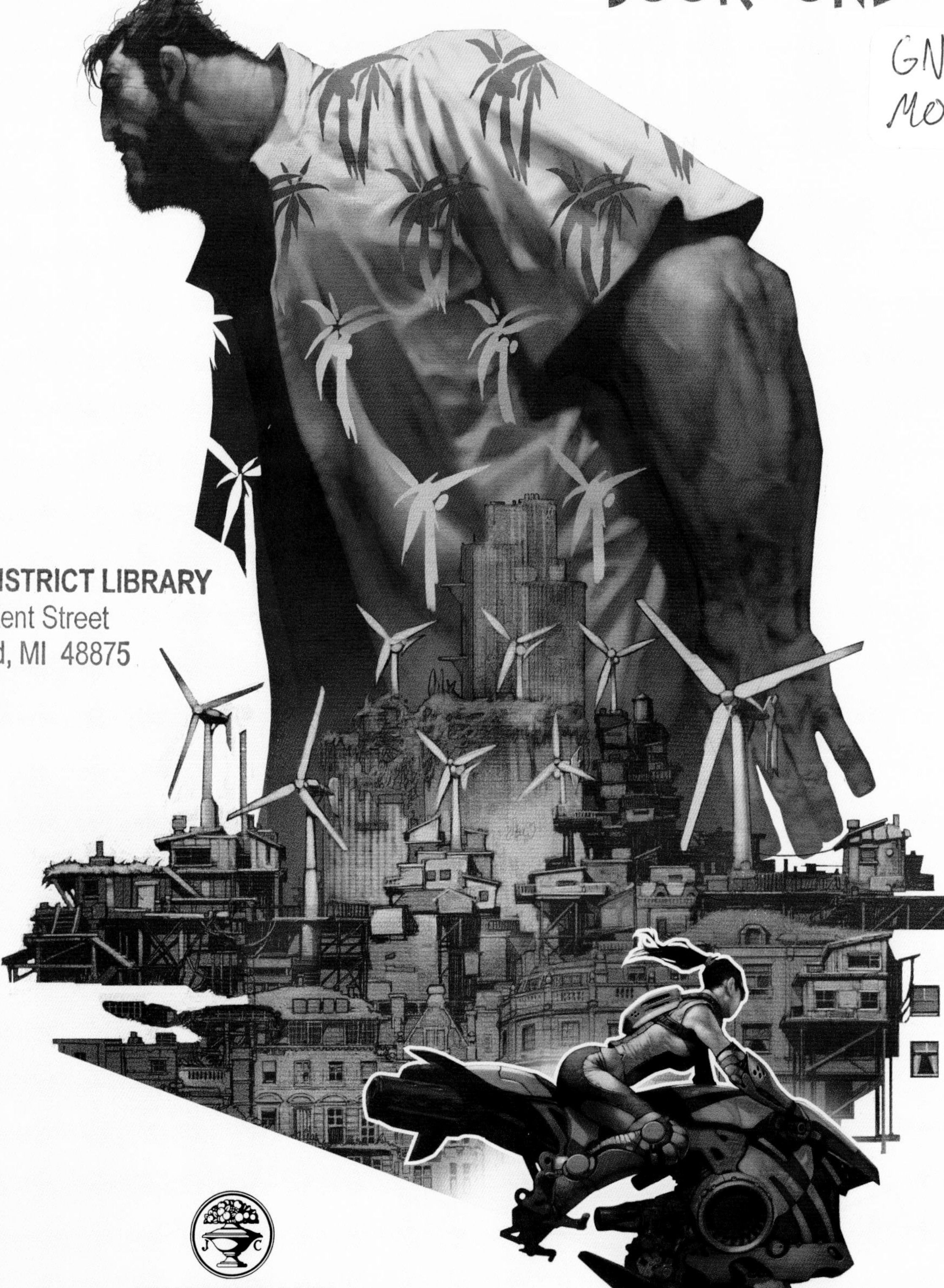



JONATHAN CAPE
LONDON

ROBBIE MORRISON JIM MURRAY

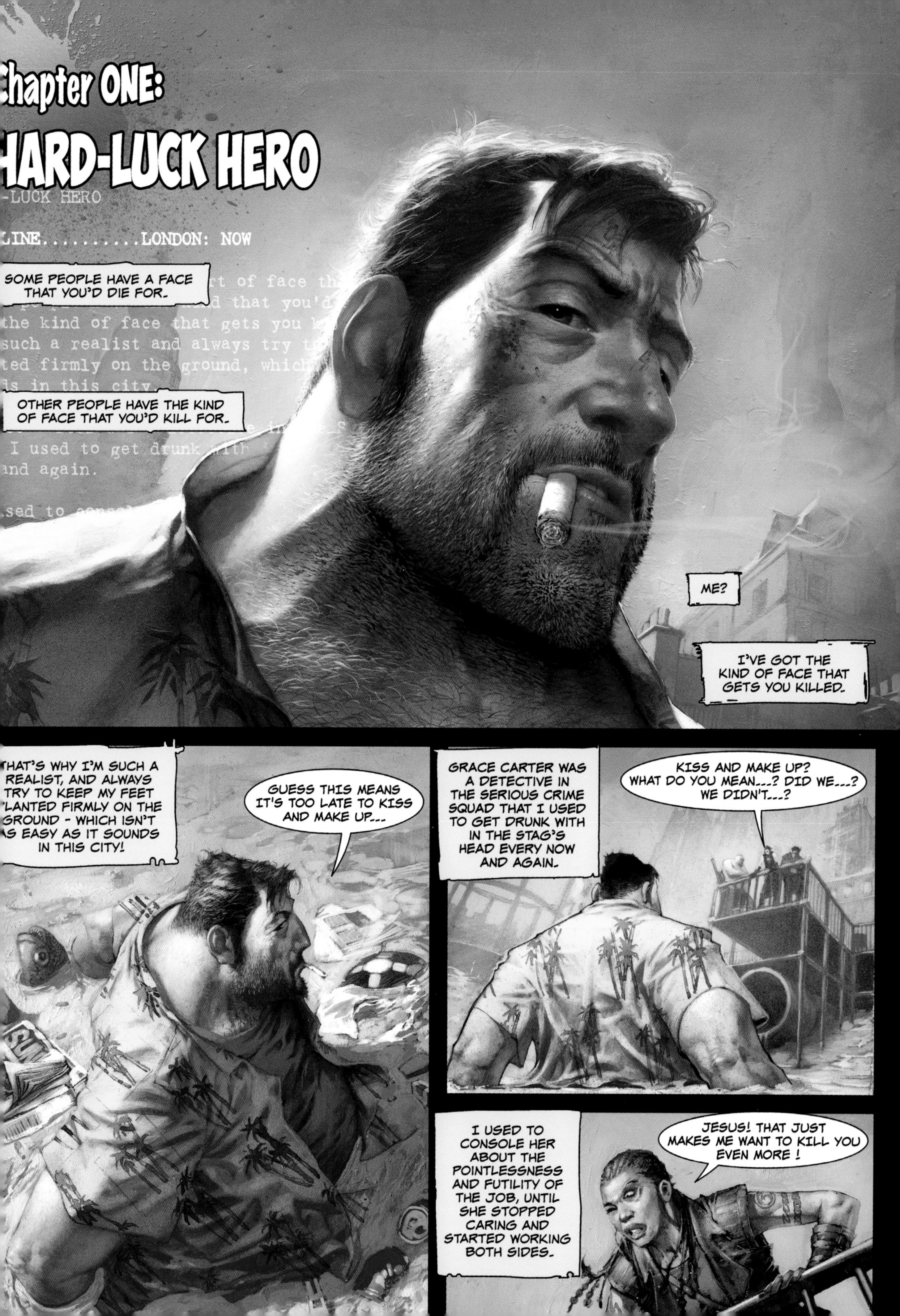
Chapter ONE:
HARD-LUCK HERO
-LUCK HERO
LINE..........LONDON: NOW
SOME PEOPLE HAVE A FACE THAT YOU'D DIE FOR.
OTHER PEOPLE HAVE THE KIND OF FACE THAT YOU'D KILL FOR.
ME?
I'VE GOT THE KIND OF FACE THAT GETS YOU KILLED.
THAT'S WHY I'M SUCH A REALIST, AND ALWAYS TRY TO KEEP MY FEET PLANTED FIRMLY ON THE GROUND - WHICH ISN'T AS EASY AS IT SOUNDS IN THIS CITY!
GUESS THIS MEANS IT'S TOO LATE TO KISS AND MAKE UP...
GRACE CARTER WAS A DETECTIVE IN THE SERIOUS CRIME SQUAD THAT I USED TO GET DRUNK WITH IN THE STAG'S HEAD EVERY NOW AND AGAIN.
KISS AND MAKE UP? WHAT DO YOU MEAN...? DID WE...? WE DIDN'T...?
I USED TO CONSOLE HER ABOUT THE POINTLESSNESS AND FUTILITY OF THE JOB, UNTIL SHE STOPPED CARING AND STARTED WORKING BOTH SIDES.
JESUS! THAT JUST MAKES ME WANT TO KILL YOU EVEN MORE !

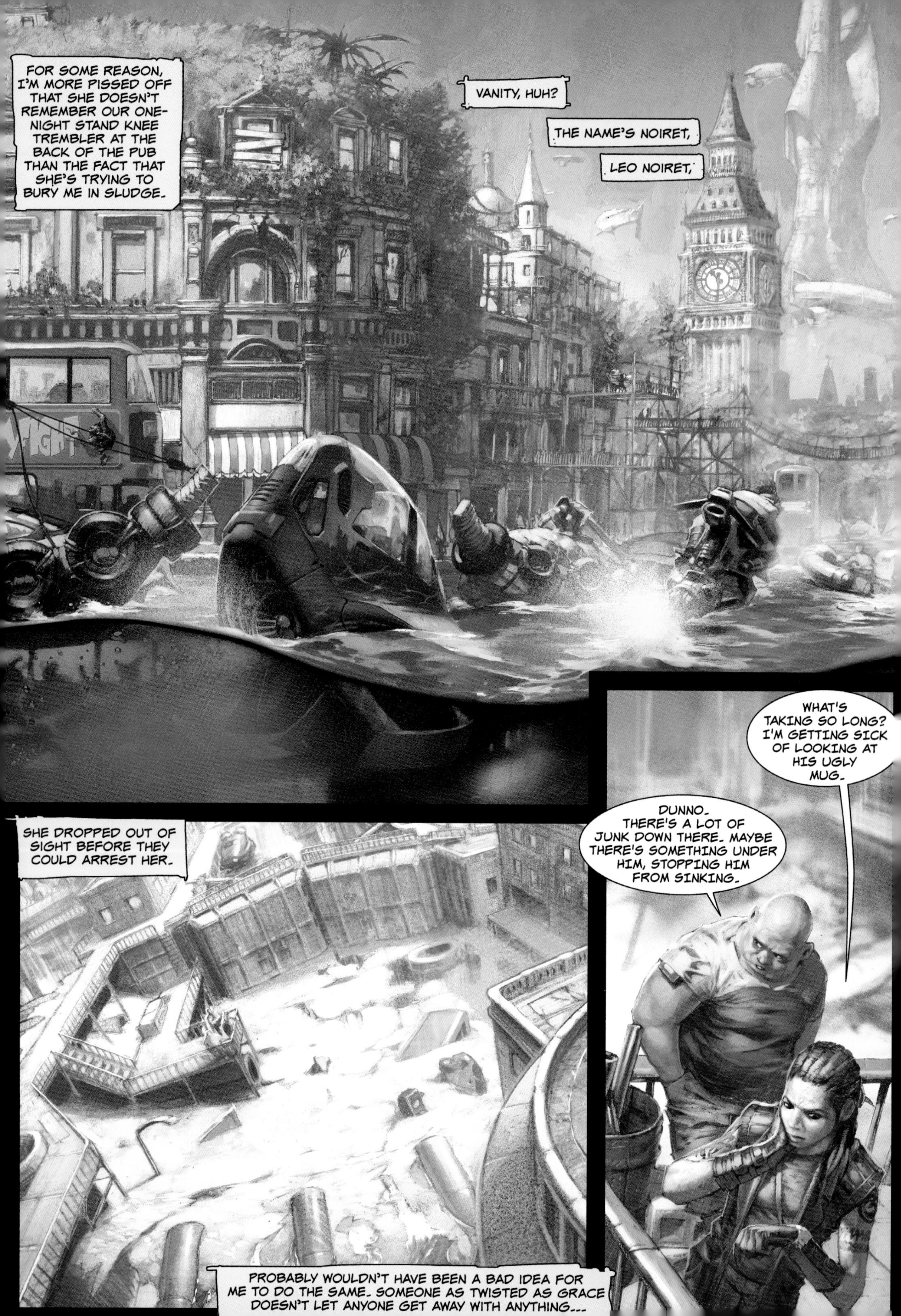

FOR SOME REASON, I'M MORE PISSED OFF THAT SHE DOESN'T REMEMBER OUR ONE-NIGHT STAND KNEE TREMBLER AT THE BACK OF THE PUB THAN THE FACT THAT SHE'S TRYING TO BURY ME IN SLUDGE.
VANITY, HUH?
THE NAME'S NOIRET,
LEO NOIRET.
SHE DROPPED OUT OF SIGHT BEFORE THEY COULD ARREST HER.
WHAT'S TAKING SO LONG? I'M GETTING SICK OF LOOKING AT HIS UGLY MUG.
DUNNO. THERE'S A LOT OF JUNK DOWN THERE. MAYBE THERE'S SOMETHING UNDER HIM, STOPPING HIM FROM SINKING.
PROBABLY WOULDN'T HAVE BEEN A BAD IDEA FOR ME TO DO THE SAME. SOMEONE AS TWISTED AS GRACE DOESN'T LET ANYONE GET AWAY WITH ANYTHING...

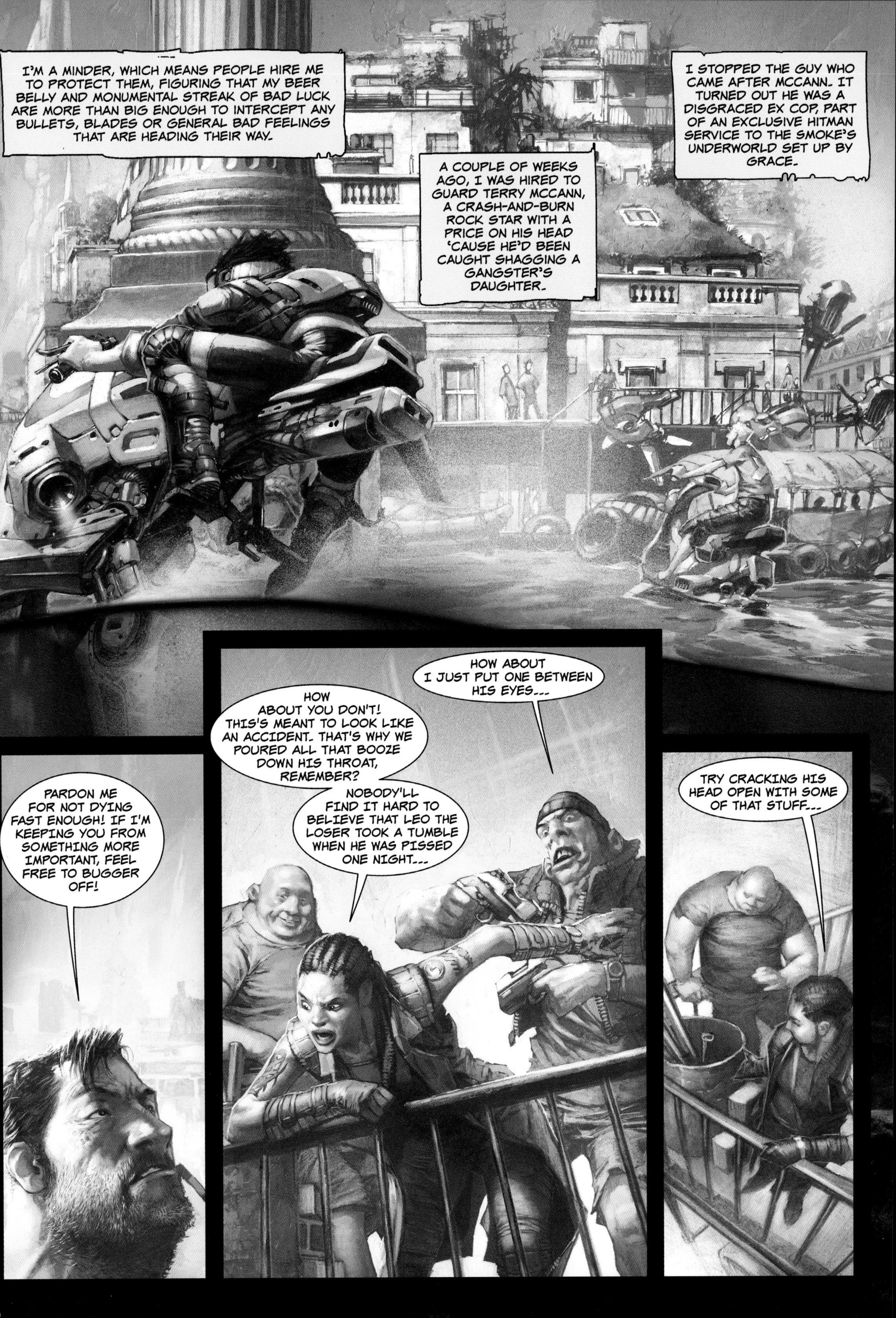
I'M A MINDER, WHICH MEANS PEOPLE HIRE ME TO PROTECT THEM, FIGURING THAT MY BEER BELLY AND MONUMENTAL STREAK OF BAD LUCK ARE MORE THAN BIG ENOUGH TO INTERCEPT ANY BULLETS, BLADES OR GENERAL BAD FEELINGS THAT ARE HEADING THEIR WAY.
A COUPLE OF WEEKS AGO, I WAS HIRED TO GUARD TERRY MCCANN, A CRASH-AND-BURN ROCK STAR WITH A PRICE ON HIS HEAD 'CAUSE HE'D BEEN CAUGHT SHAGGING A GANGSTER'S DAUGHTER.
I STOPPED THE GUY WHO CAME AFTER MCCANN. IT TURNED OUT HE WAS A DISGRACED EX COP, PART OF AN EXCLUSIVE HITMAN SERVICE TO THE SMOKE'S UNDERWORLD SET UP BY GRACE.
PARDON ME FOR NOT DYING FAST ENOUGH! IF I'M KEEPING YOU FROM SOMETHING MORE IMPORTANT, FEEL FREE TO BUGGER OFF!
HOW ABOUT I JUST PUT ONE BETWEEN HIS EYES...
HOW ABOUT YOU DON'T! THIS'S MEANT TO LOOK LIKE AN ACCIDENT. THAT'S WHY WE POURED ALL THAT BOOZE DOWN HIS THROAT, REMEMBER?
NOBODY'LL FIND IT HARD TO BELIEVE THAT LEO THE LOSER TOOK A TUMBLE WHEN HE WAS PISSED ONE NIGHT...
TRY CRACKING HIS HEAD OPEN WITH SOME OF THAT STUFF...

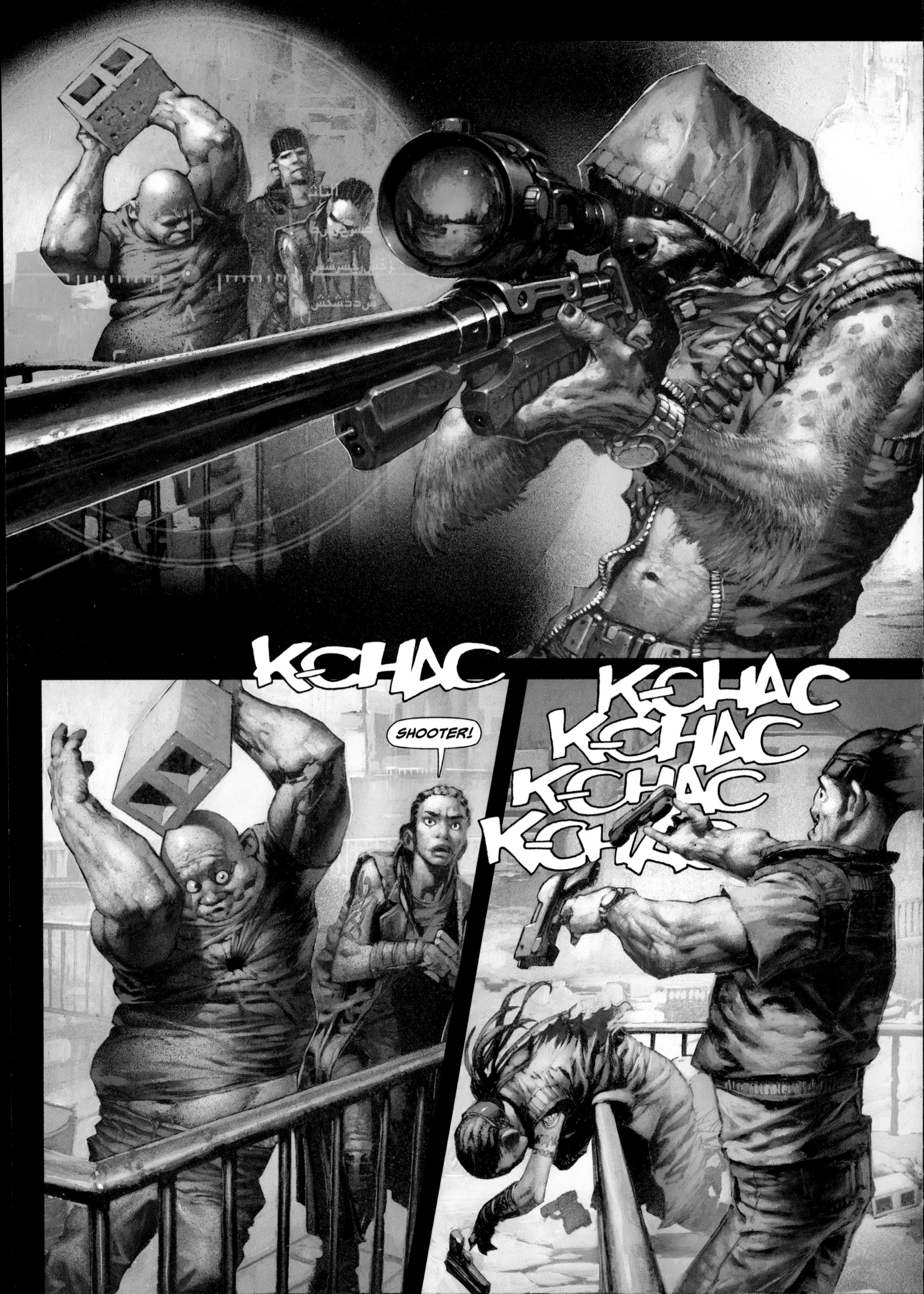
K-CHAC
SHOOTER!
K-CHAC
K-CHAC
K-CHAC

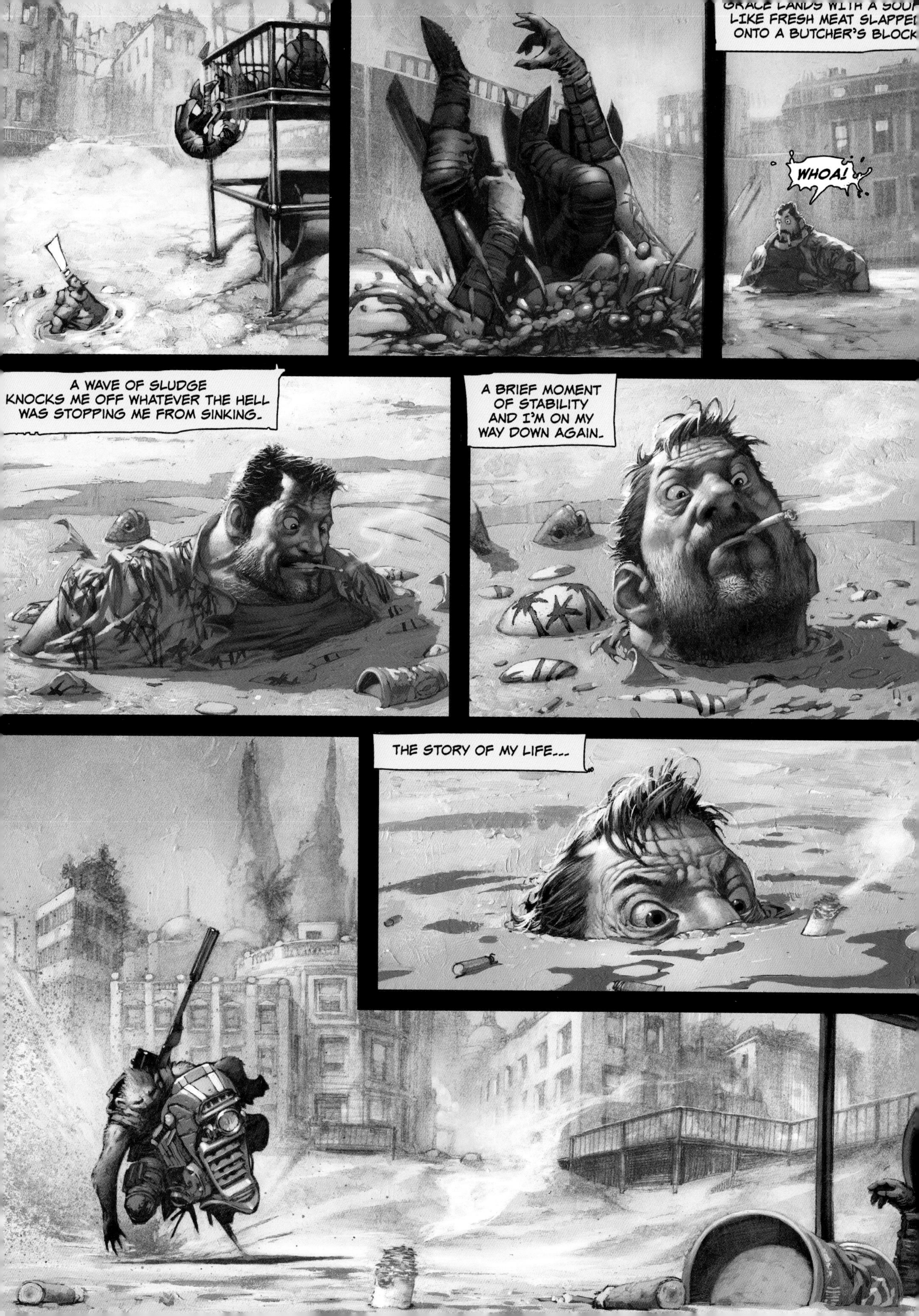
LIKE FRESH MEAT SLAPPED
ONTO A BUTCHER'S BLOCK
WHOA!
A WAVE OF SLUDGE KNOCKS ME OFF WHATEVER THE HELL WAS STOPPING ME FROM SINKING.
A BRIEF MOMENT OF STABILITY AND I'M ON MY WAY DOWN AGAIN.
THE STORY OF MY LIFE...

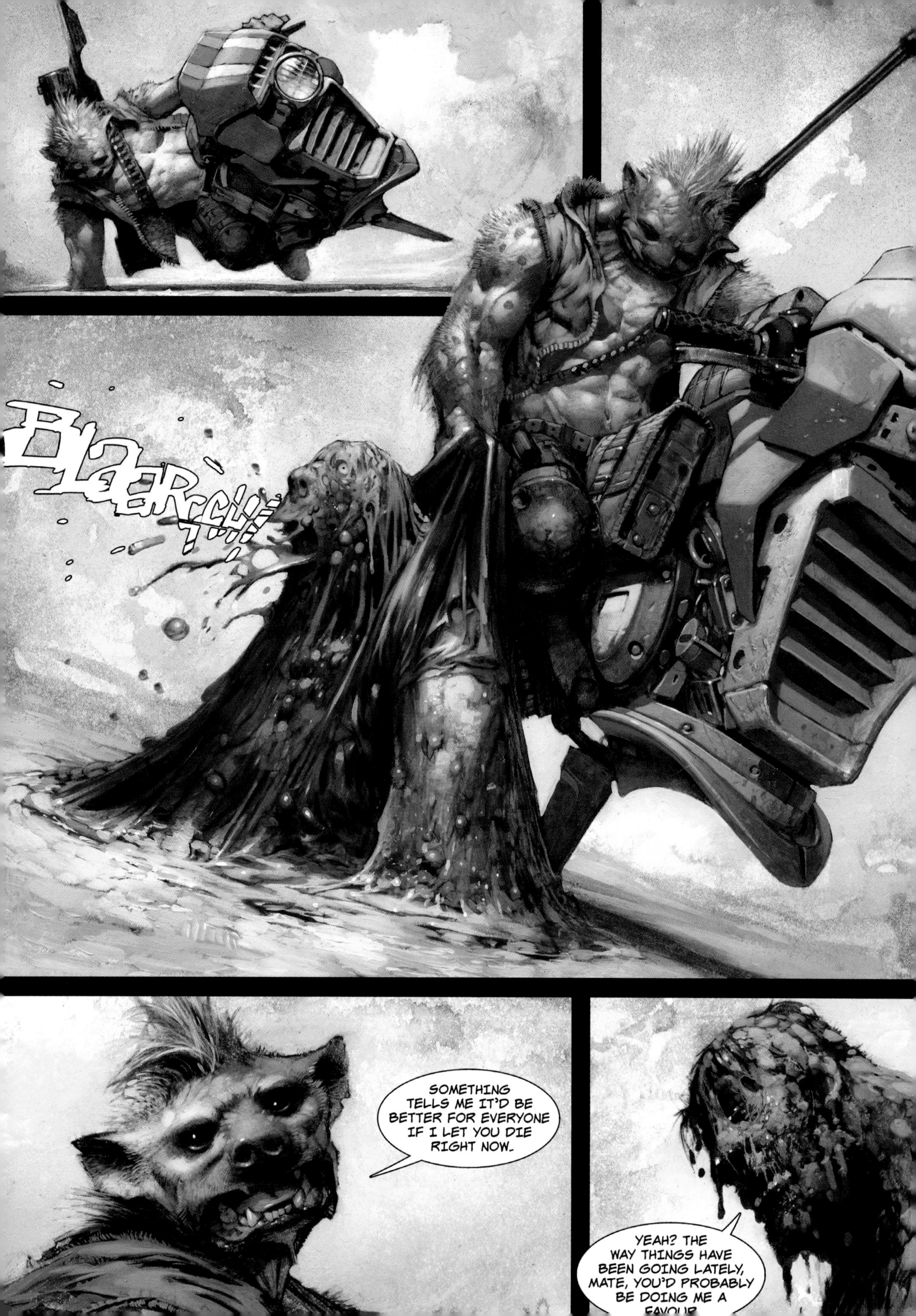
BLAARGGH!!!
SOMETHING TELLS ME IT'D BE BETTER FOR EVERYONE IF I LET YOU DIE RIGHT NOW.
YEAH? THE WAY THINGS HAVE BEEN GOING LATELY, MATE, YOU'D PROBABLY BE DOING ME A FAVOUR.

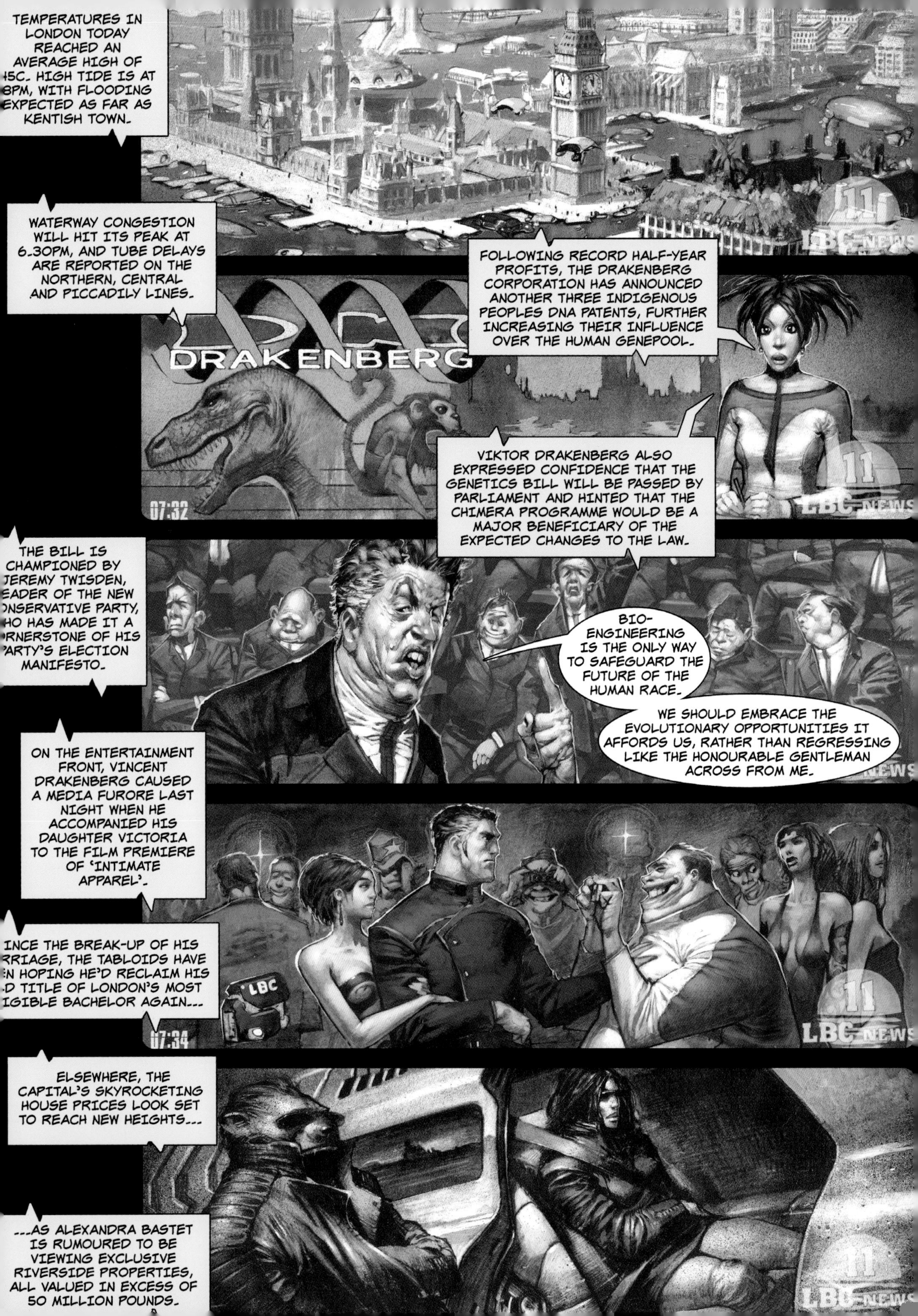
TEMPERATURES IN LONDON TODAY REACHED AN AVERAGE HIGH OF 45C. HIGH TIDE IS AT 8PM, WITH FLOODING EXPECTED AS FAR AS KENTISH TOWN.
WATERWAY CONGESTION WILL HIT ITS PEAK AT 6.30PM, AND TUBE DELAYS ARE REPORTED ON THE NORTHERN, CENTRAL AND PICCADILY LINES.
11 LBC NEWS
DRAKENBERG
FOLLOWING RECORD HALF-YEAR PROFITS, THE DRAKENBERG CORPORATION HAS ANNOUNCED ANOTHER THREE INDIGENOUS PEOPLES DNA PATENTS, FURTHER INCREASING THEIR INFLUENCE OVER THE HUMAN GENEPOOL.
VIKTOR DRAKENBERG ALSO EXPRESSED CONFIDENCE THAT THE GENETICS BILL WILL BE PASSED BY PARLIAMENT AND HINTED THAT THE CHIMERA PROGRAMME WOULD BE A MAJOR BENEFICIARY OF THE EXPECTED CHANGES TO THE LAW.
07:32
11 LBC NEWS
THE BILL IS CHAMPIONED BY JEREMY TWISDEN, EADER OF THE NEW ONSERVATIVE PARTY, HO HAS MADE IT A RNERSTONE OF HIS ARTY'S ELECTION MANIFESTO.
BIO-ENGINEERING IS THE ONLY WAY TO SAFEGUARD THE FUTURE OF THE HUMAN RACE.
WE SHOULD EMBRACE THE EVOLUTIONARY OPPORTUNITIES IT AFFORDS US, RATHER THAN REGRESSING LIKE THE HONOURABLE GENTLEMAN ACROSS FROM ME.
ON THE ENTERTAINMENT FRONT, VINCENT DRAKENBERG CAUSED A MEDIA FURORE LAST NIGHT WHEN HE ACCOMPANIED HIS DAUGHTER VICTORIA TO THE FILM PREMIERE OF 'INTIMATE APPAREL'.
INCE THE BREAK-UP OF HIS RRIAGE, THE TABLOIDS HAVE EN HOPING HE'D RECLAIM HIS D TITLE OF LONDON'S MOST IGIBLE BACHELOR AGAIN...
LBC
07:34
11 LBC NEWS
ELSEWHERE, THE CAPITAL'S SKYROCKETING HOUSE PRICES LOOK SET TO REACH NEW HEIGHTS...
...AS ALEXANDRA BASTET IS RUMOURED TO BE VIEWING EXCLUSIVE RIVERSIDE PROPERTIES, ALL VALUED IN EXCESS OF 50 MILLION POUNDS.
11 LBC NEWS

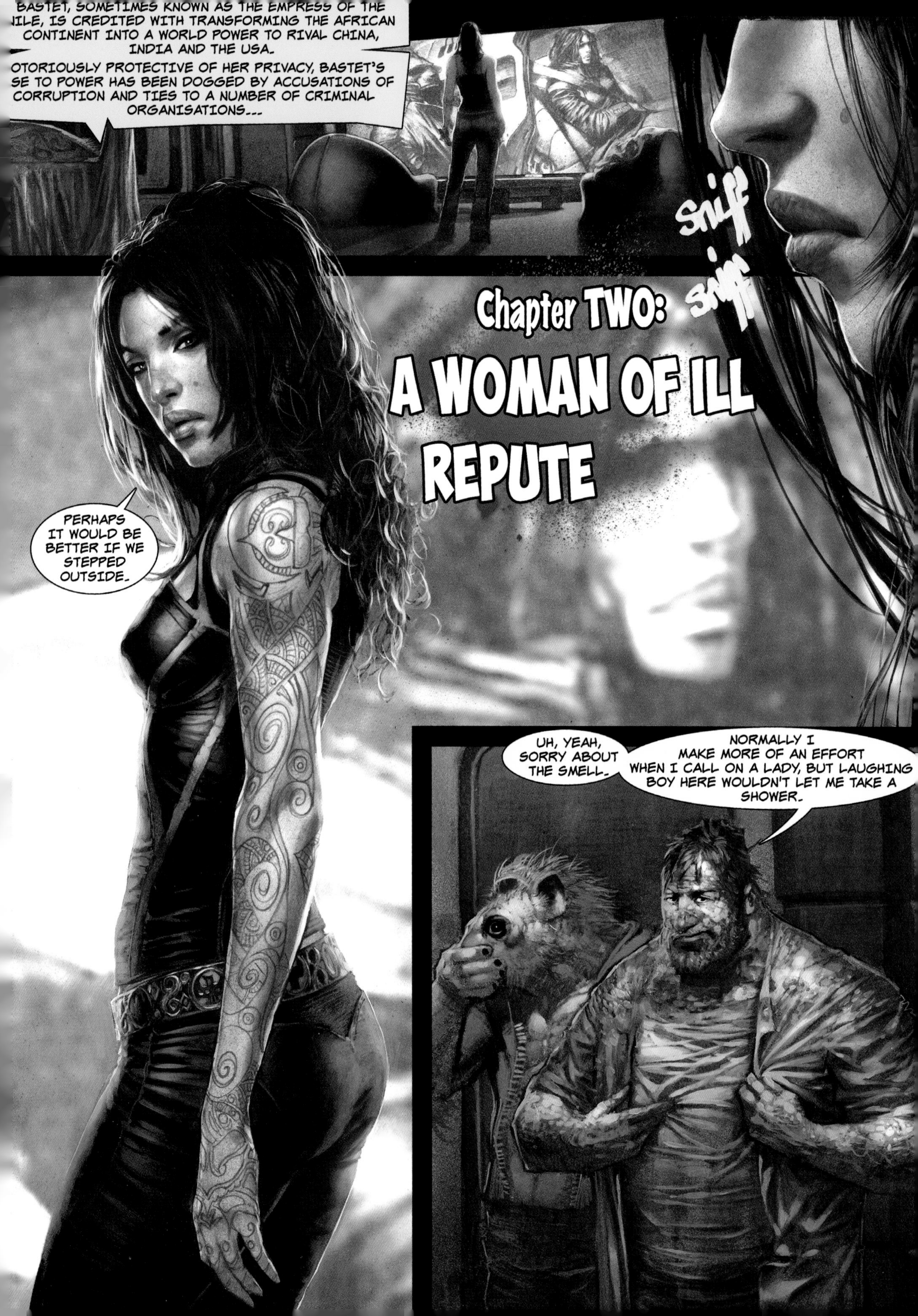
BASTET, SOMETIMES KNOWN AS THE EMPRESS OF THE NILE, IS CREDITED WITH TRANSFORMING THE AFRICAN CONTINENT INTO A WORLD POWER TO RIVAL CHINA, INDIA AND THE USA.
OTORIOUSLY PROTECTIVE OF HER PRIVACY, BASTET'S SE TO POWER HAS BEEN DOGGED BY ACCUSATIONS OF CORRUPTION AND TIES TO A NUMBER OF CRIMINAL ORGANISATIONS...
SNIFF
SNIFF
Chapter TWO:
A WOMAN OF ILL REPUTE
PERHAPS IT WOULD BE BETTER IF WE STEPPED OUTSIDE.
UH, YEAH, SORRY ABOUT THE SMELL.
NORMALLY I MAKE MORE OF AN EFFORT WHEN I CALL ON A LADY, BUT LAUGHING BOY HERE WOULDN'T LET ME TAKE A SHOWER.

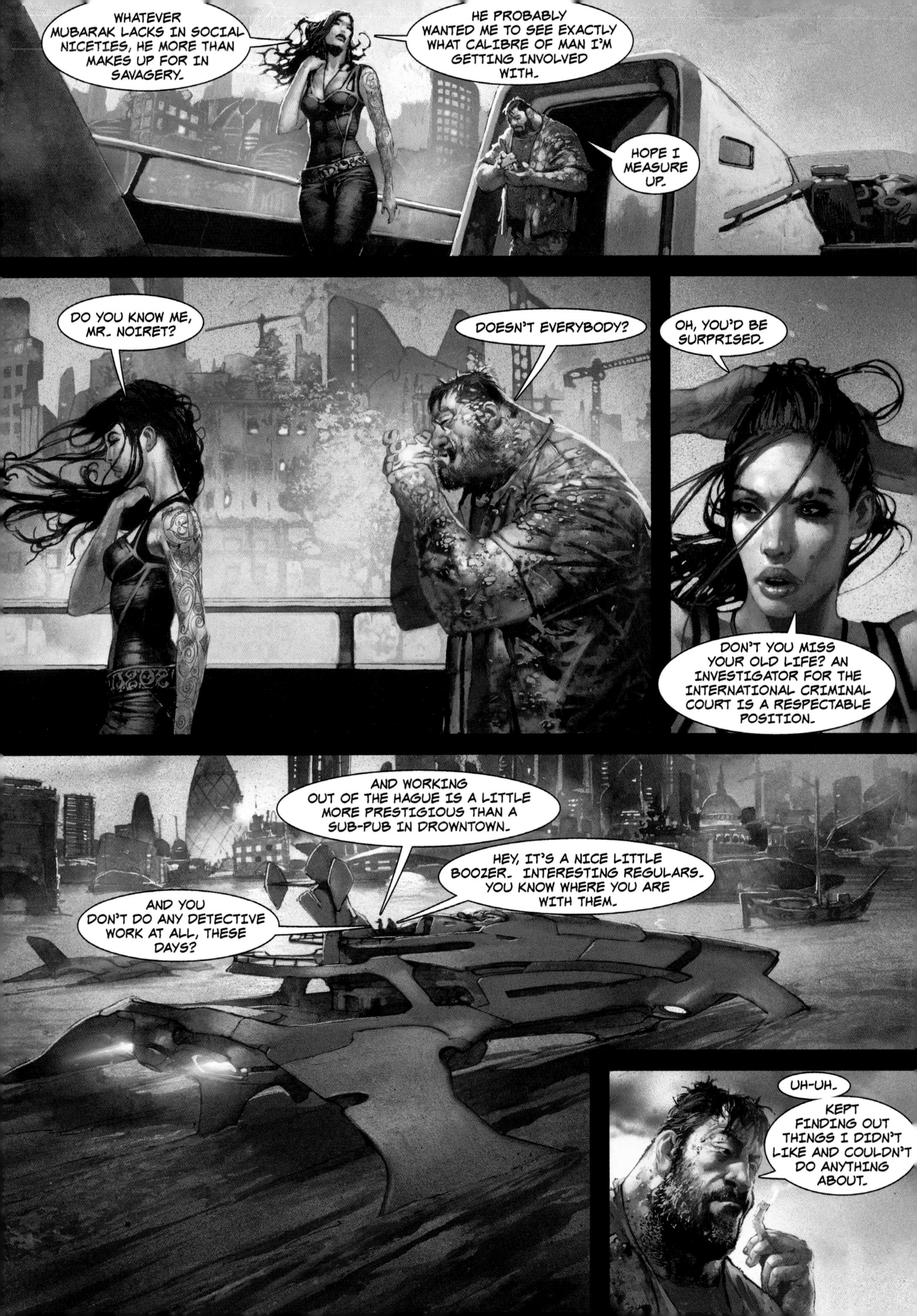
WHATEVER MUBARAK LACKS IN SOCIAL NICETIES, HE MORE THAN MAKES UP FOR IN SAVAGERY.
HE PROBABLY WANTED ME TO SEE EXACTLY WHAT CALIBRE OF MAN I'M GETTING INVOLVED WITH.
HOPE I MEASURE UP.
DO YOU KNOW ME, MR. NOIRET?
DOESN'T EVERYBODY?
OH, YOU'D BE SURPRISED.
DON'T YOU MISS YOUR OLD LIFE? AN INVESTIGATOR FOR THE INTERNATIONAL CRIMINAL COURT IS A RESPECTABLE POSITION.
AND WORKING OUT OF THE HAGUE IS A LITTLE MORE PRESTIGIOUS THAN A SUB-PUB IN DROWNTOWN.
HEY, IT'S A NICE LITTLE BOOZER. INTERESTING REGULARS. YOU KNOW WHERE YOU ARE WITH THEM.
AND YOU DON'T DO ANY DETECTIVE WORK AT ALL, THESE DAYS?
UH-UH.
KEPT FINDING OUT THINGS I DIDN'T LIKE AND COULDN'T DO ANYTHING ABOUT.

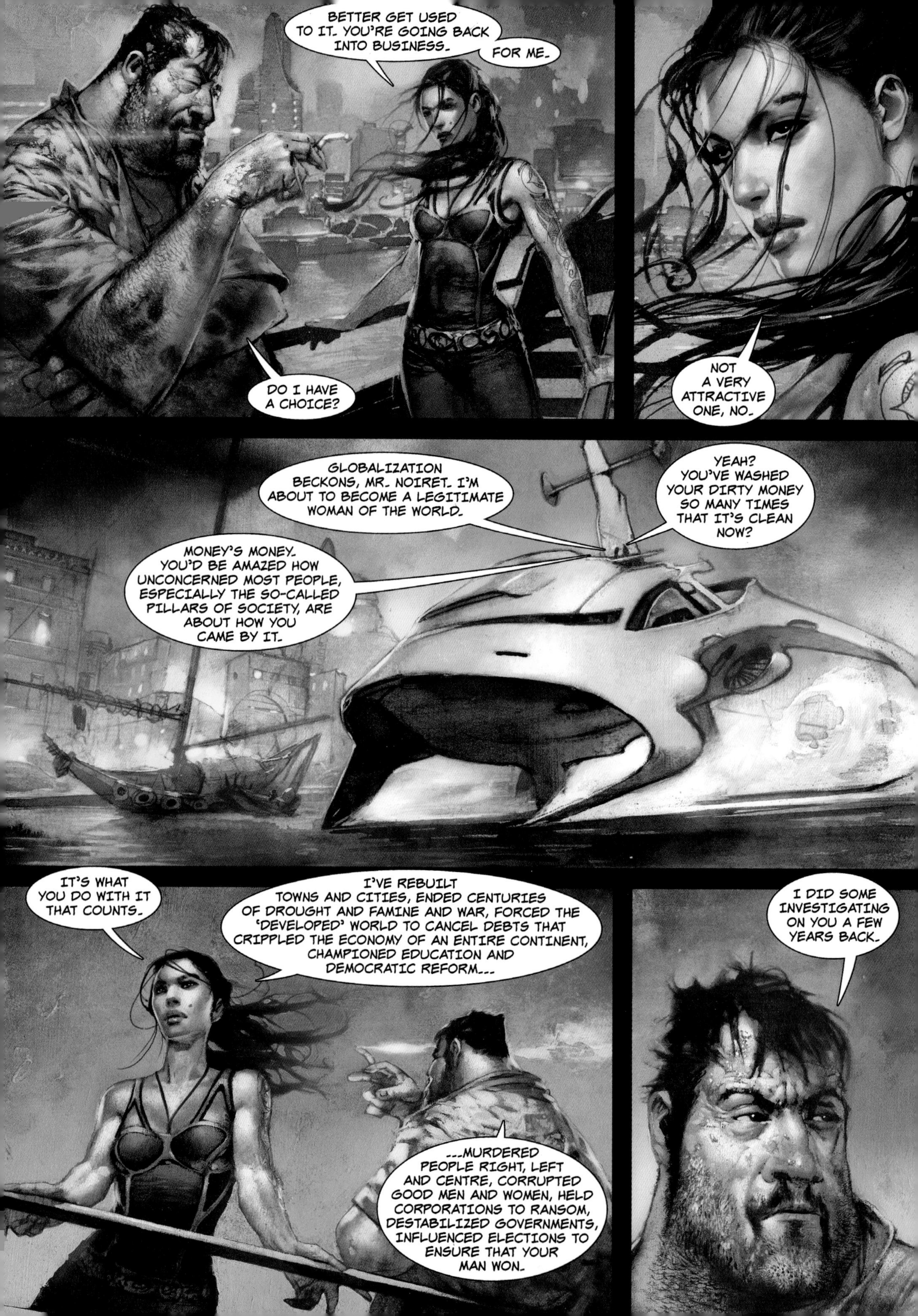

BETTER GET USED TO IT. YOU'RE GOING BACK INTO BUSINESS.
FOR ME.
DO I HAVE A CHOICE?
NOT A VERY ATTRACTIVE ONE, NO.
GLOBALIZATION BECKONS, MR. NOIRET. I'M ABOUT TO BECOME A LEGITIMATE WOMAN OF THE WORLD.
YEAH? YOU'VE WASHED YOUR DIRTY MONEY SO MANY TIMES THAT IT'S CLEAN NOW?
MONEY'S MONEY. YOU'D BE AMAZED HOW UNCONCERNED MOST PEOPLE, ESPECIALLY THE SO-CALLED PILLARS OF SOCIETY, ARE ABOUT HOW YOU CAME BY IT.
IT'S WHAT YOU DO WITH IT THAT COUNTS.
I'VE REBUILT TOWNS AND CITIES, ENDED CENTURIES OF DROUGHT AND FAMINE AND WAR, FORCED THE 'DEVELOPED' WORLD TO CANCEL DEBTS THAT CRIPPLED THE ECONOMY OF AN ENTIRE CONTINENT, CHAMPIONED EDUCATION AND DEMOCRATIC REFORM...
...MURDERED PEOPLE RIGHT, LEFT AND CENTRE, CORRUPTED GOOD MEN AND WOMEN, HELD CORPORATIONS TO RANSOM, DESTABILIZED GOVERNMENTS, INFLUENCED ELECTIONS TO ENSURE THAT YOUR MAN WON.
I DID SOME INVESTIGATING ON YOU A FEW YEARS BACK.

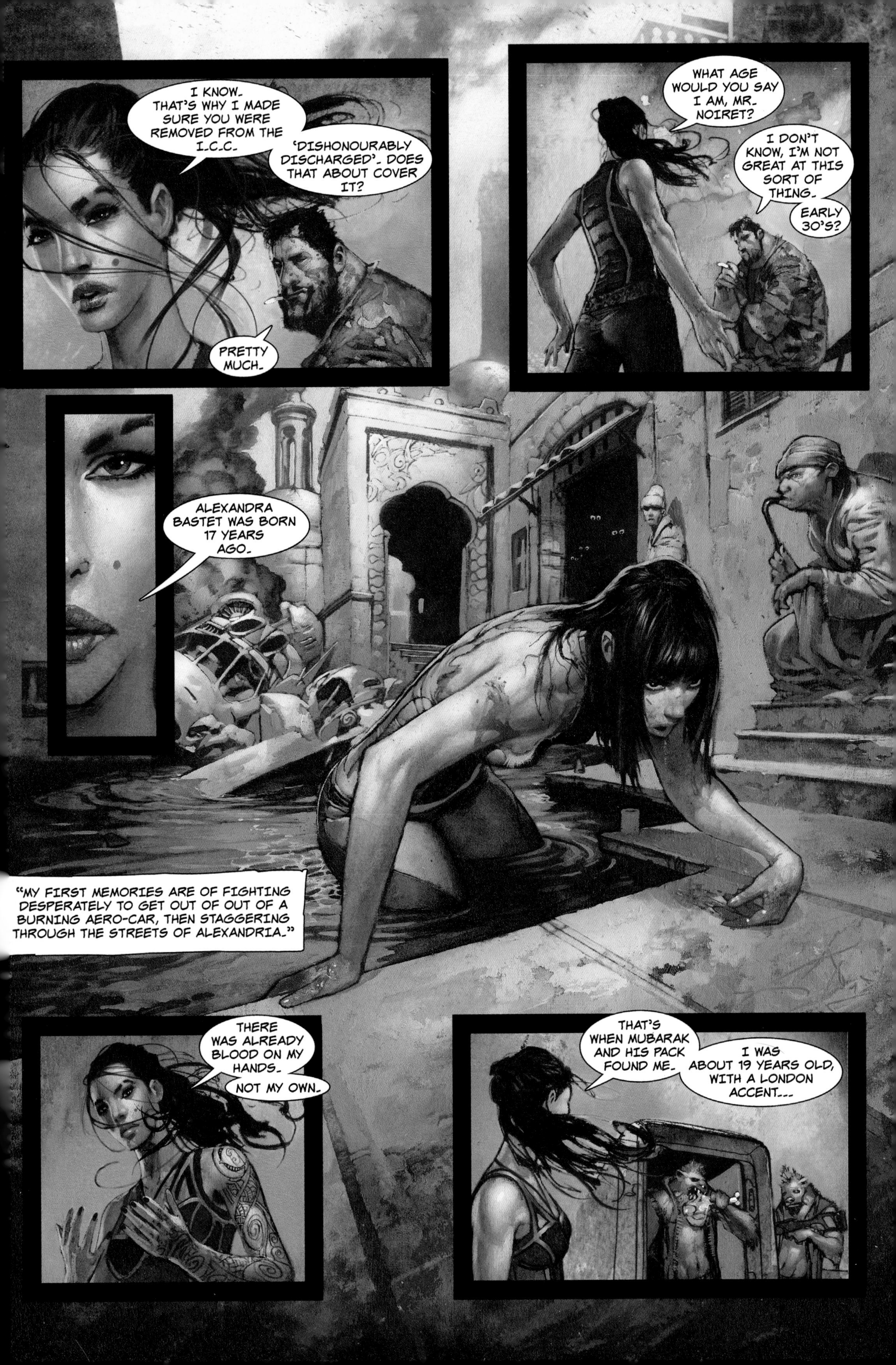
I KNOW. THAT'S WHY I MADE SURE YOU WERE REMOVED FROM THE I.C.C.
'DISHONOURABLY DISCHARGED'. DOES THAT ABOUT COVER IT?
PRETTY MUCH.
WHAT AGE WOULD YOU SAY I AM, MR. NOIRET?
I DON'T KNOW, I'M NOT GREAT AT THIS SORT OF THING.
EARLY 30'S?
ALEXANDRA BASTET WAS BORN 17 YEARS AGO.
"MY FIRST MEMORIES ARE OF FIGHTING DESPERATELY TO GET OUT OF OUT OF A BURNING AERO-CAR, THEN STAGGERING THROUGH THE STREETS OF ALEXANDRIA."
THERE WAS ALREADY BLOOD ON MY HANDS.
NOT MY OWN.
THAT'S WHEN MUBARAK AND HIS PACK FOUND ME.
I WAS ABOUT 19 YEARS OLD, WITH A LONDON ACCENT...

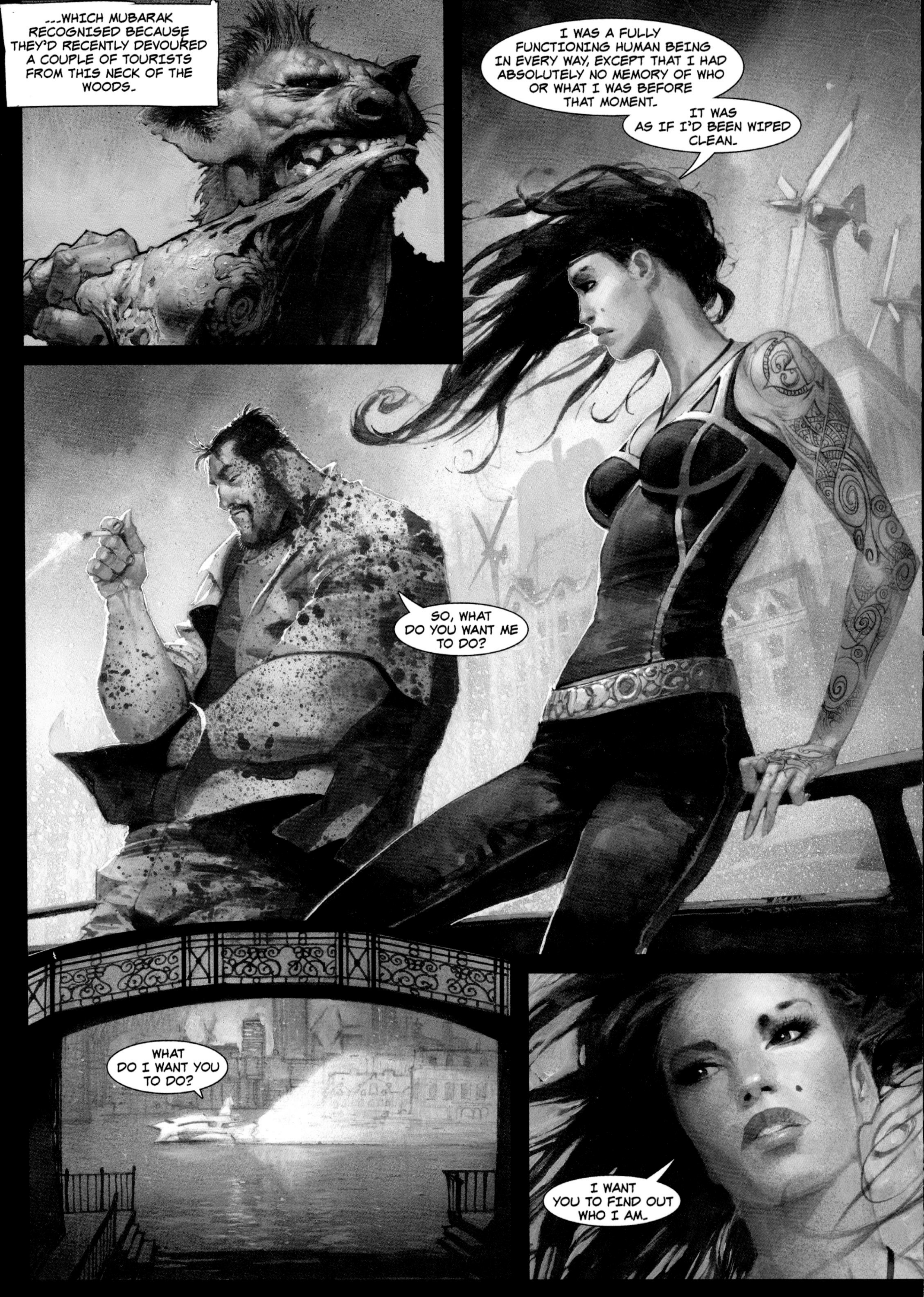
...WHICH MUBARAK RECOGNISED BECAUSE THEY'D RECENTLY DEVOURED A COUPLE OF TOURISTS FROM THIS NECK OF THE WOODS.
I WAS A FULLY FUNCTIONING HUMAN BEING IN EVERY WAY, EXCEPT THAT I HAD ABSOLUTELY NO MEMORY OF WHO OR WHAT I WAS BEFORE THAT MOMENT.
IT WAS AS IF I'D BEEN WIPED CLEAN.
SO, WHAT DO YOU WANT ME TO DO?
WHAT DO I WANT YOU TO DO?
I WANT YOU TO FIND OUT WHO I AM.

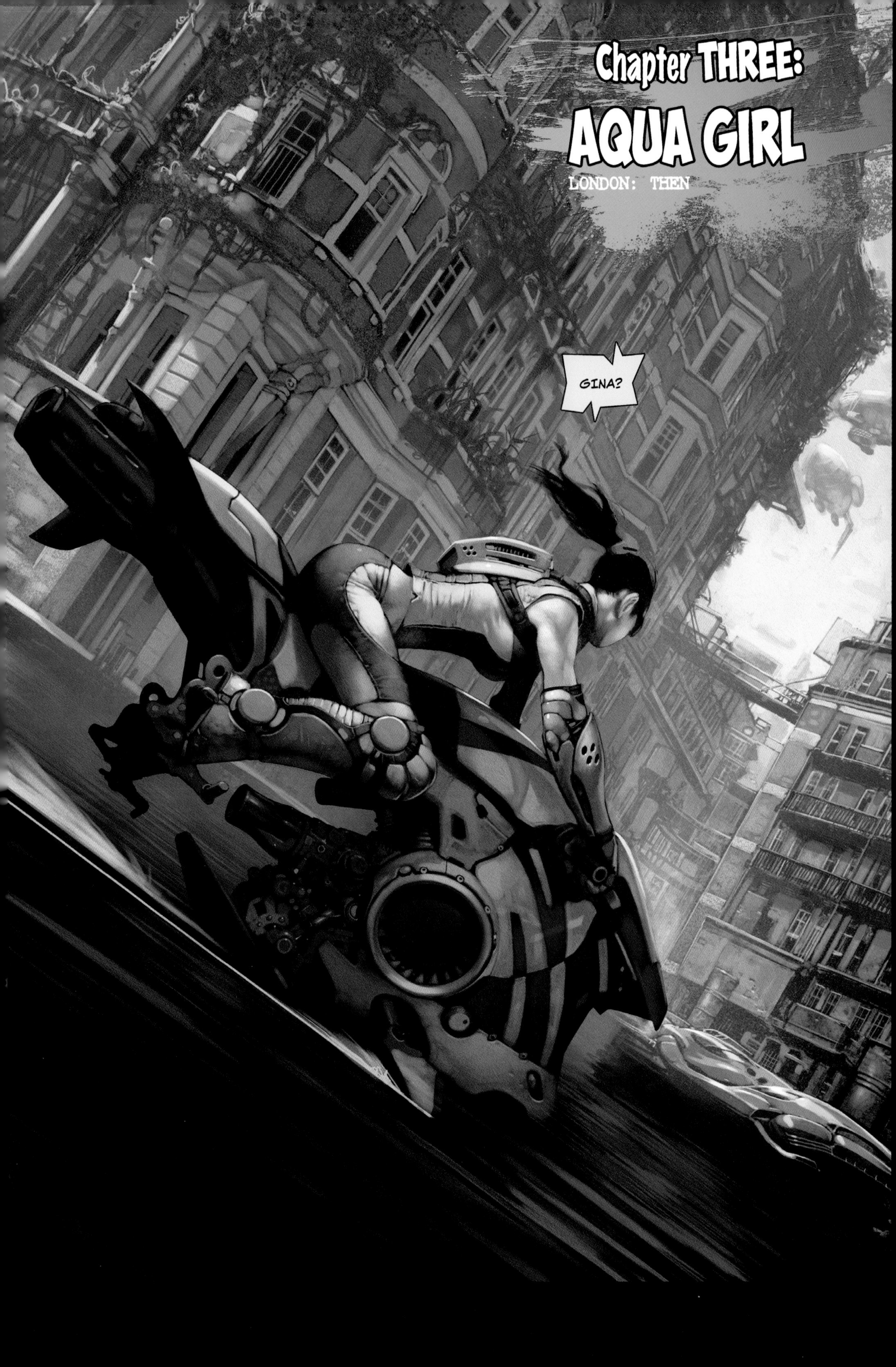
Chapter THREE:
AQUA GIRL
LONDON: THEN
GINA?

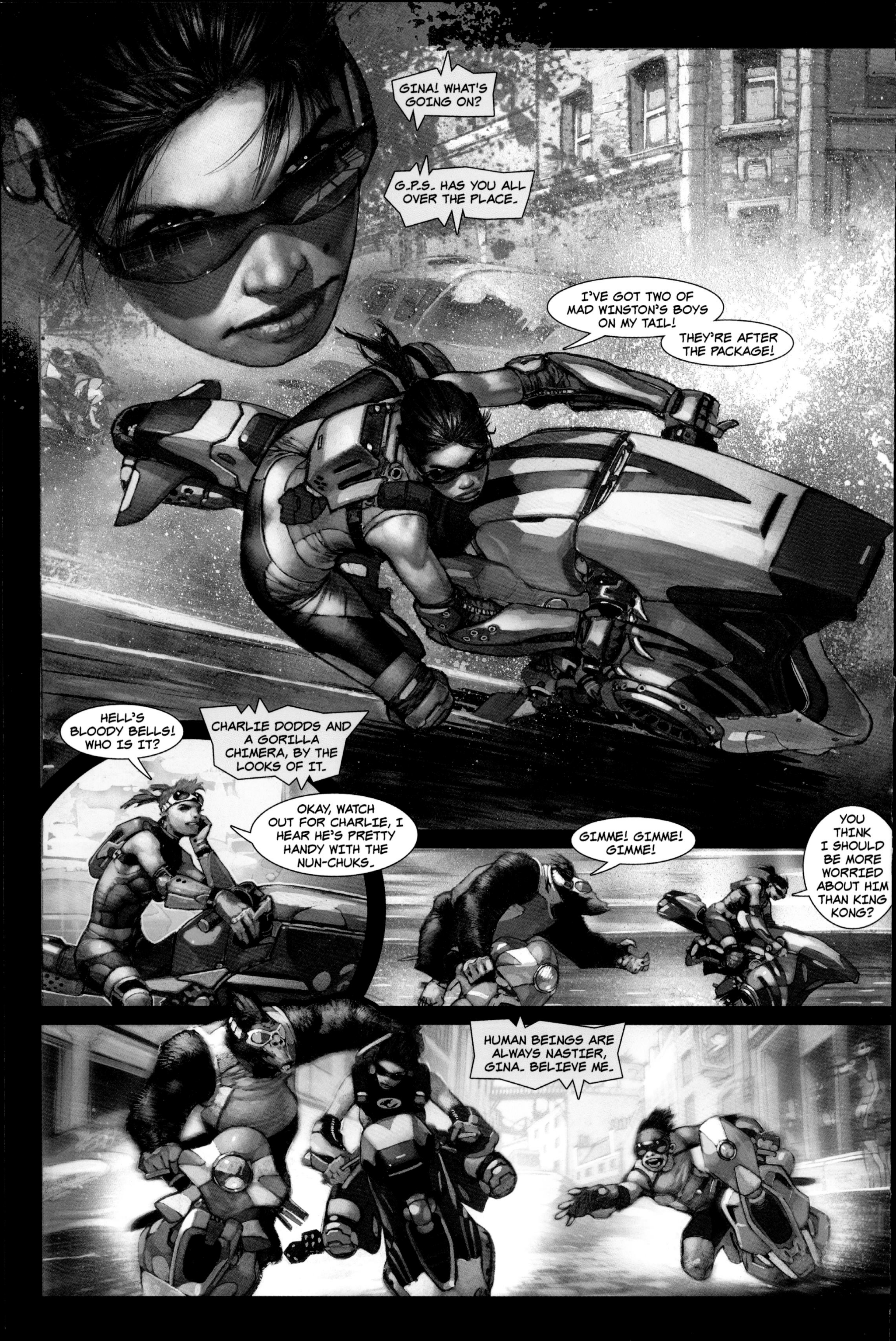
GINA! WHAT'S GOING ON?
G.P.S. HAS YOU ALL OVER THE PLACE.
I'VE GOT TWO OF MAD WINSTON'S BOYS ON MY TAIL!
THEY'RE AFTER THE PACKAGE!
HELL'S BLOODY BELLS! WHO IS IT?
CHARLIE DODDS AND A GORILLA CHIMERA, BY THE LOOKS OF IT.
OKAY, WATCH OUT FOR CHARLIE, I HEAR HE'S PRETTY HANDY WITH THE NUN-CHUKS.
GIMME! GIMME! GIMME!
YOU THINK I SHOULD BE MORE WORRIED ABOUT HIM THAN KING KONG?
HUMAN BEINGS ARE ALWAYS NASTIER, GINA. BELIEVE ME.

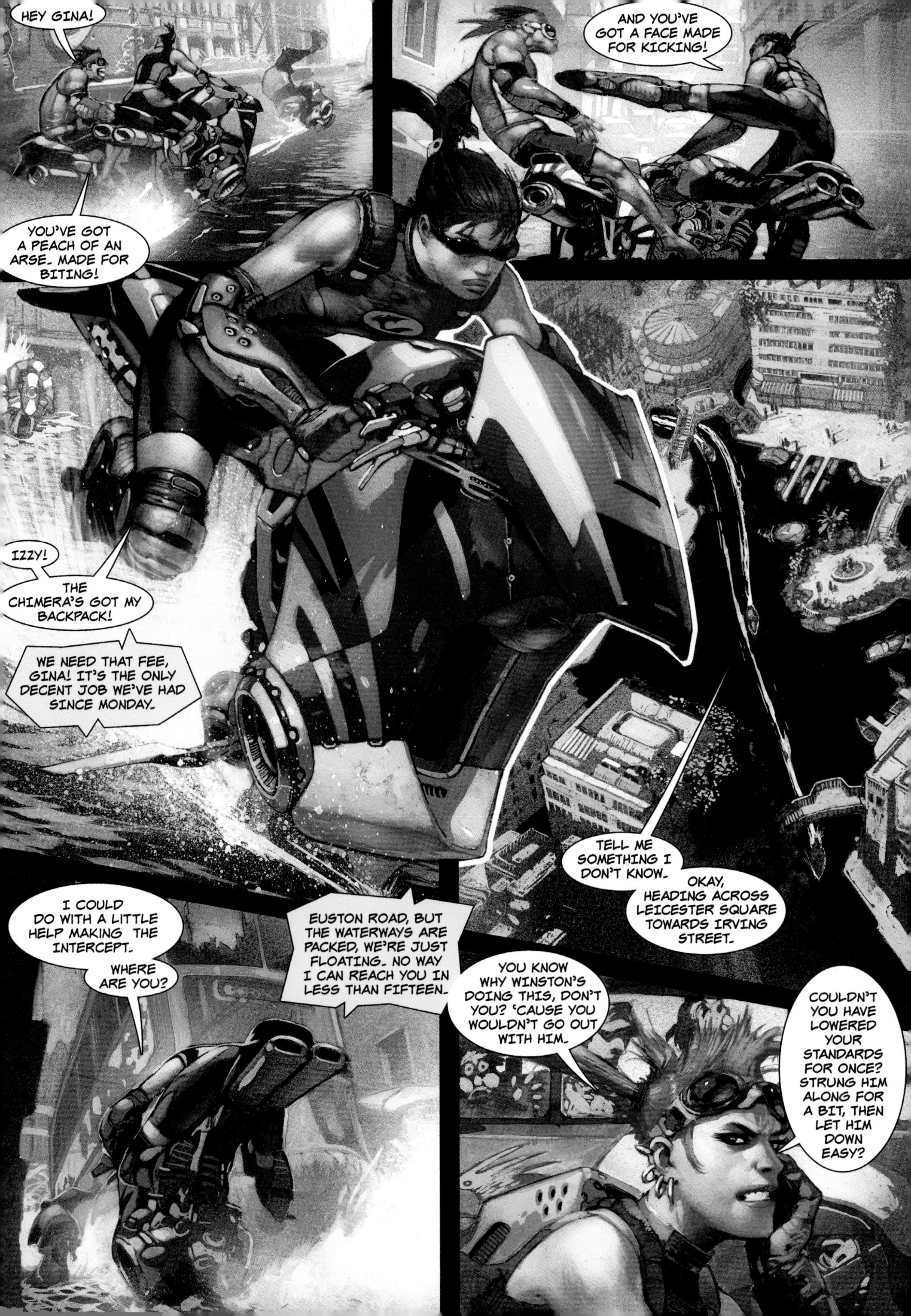
HEY GINA!
YOU'VE GOT A PEACH OF AN ARSE. MADE FOR BITING!
AND YOU'VE GOT A FACE MADE FOR KICKING!
IZZY!
THE CHIMERA'S GOT MY BACKPACK!
WE NEED THAT FEE, GINA! IT'S THE ONLY DECENT JOB WE'VE HAD SINCE MONDAY.
TELL ME SOMETHING I DON'T KNOW.
OKAY, HEADING ACROSS LEICESTER SQUARE TOWARDS IRVING STREET.
I COULD DO WITH A LITTLE HELP MAKING THE INTERCEPT.
WHERE ARE YOU?
EUSTON ROAD, BUT THE WATERWAYS ARE PACKED, WE'RE JUST FLOATING. NO WAY I CAN REACH YOU IN LESS THAN FIFTEEN.
YOU KNOW WHY WINSTON'S DOING THIS, DON'T YOU? 'CAUSE YOU WOULDN'T GO OUT WITH HIM.
COULDN'T YOU HAVE LOWERED YOUR STANDARDS FOR ONCE? STRUNG HIM ALONG FOR A BIT, THEN LET HIM DOWN EASY?

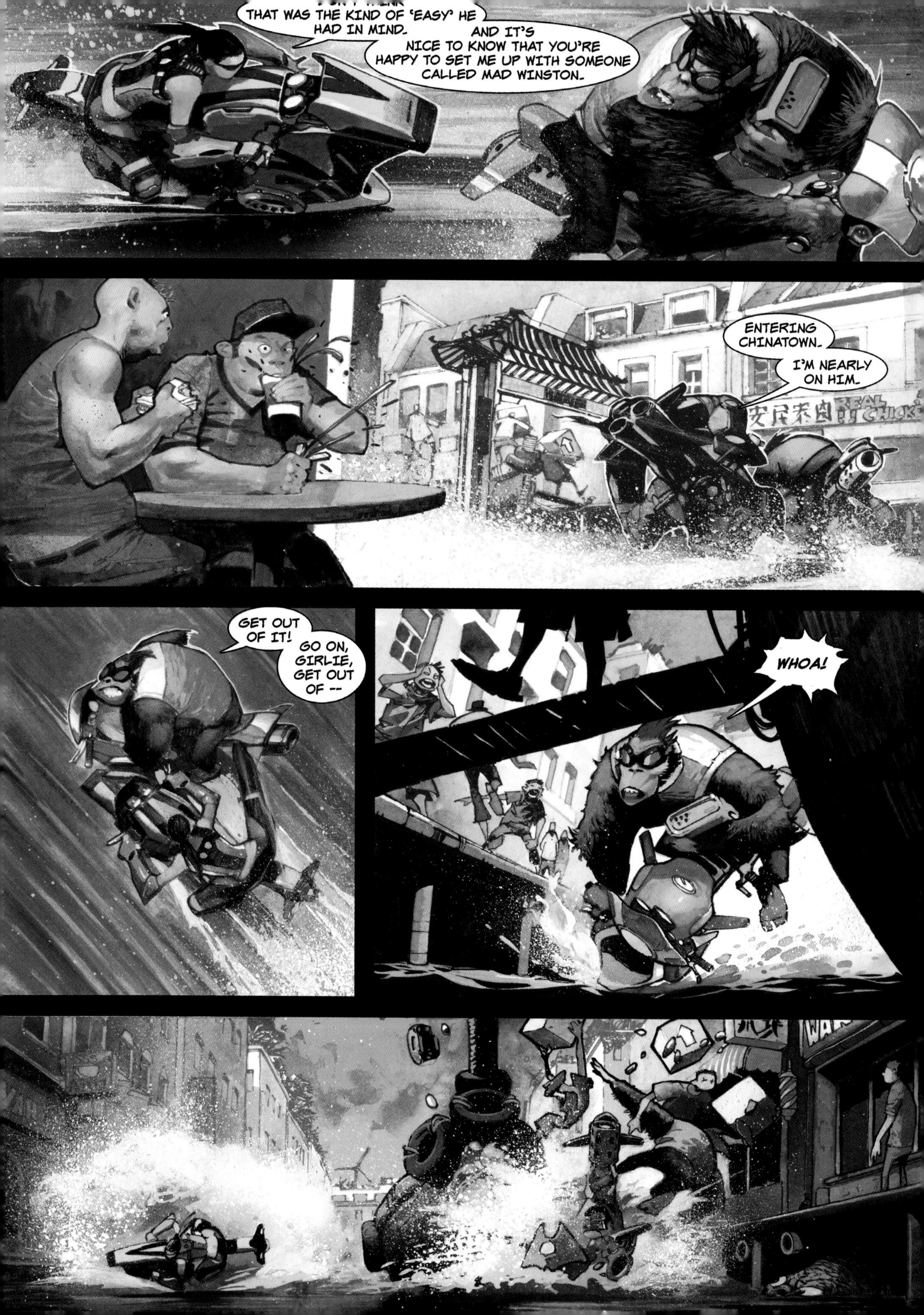
THAT WAS THE KIND OF 'EASY' HE HAD IN MIND.
AND IT'S NICE TO KNOW THAT YOU'RE HAPPY TO SET ME UP WITH SOMEONE CALLED MAD WINSTON.
ENTERING CHINATOWN.
I'M NEARLY ON HIM.
GET OUT OF IT!
GO ON, GIRLIE, GET OUT OF --
WHOA!

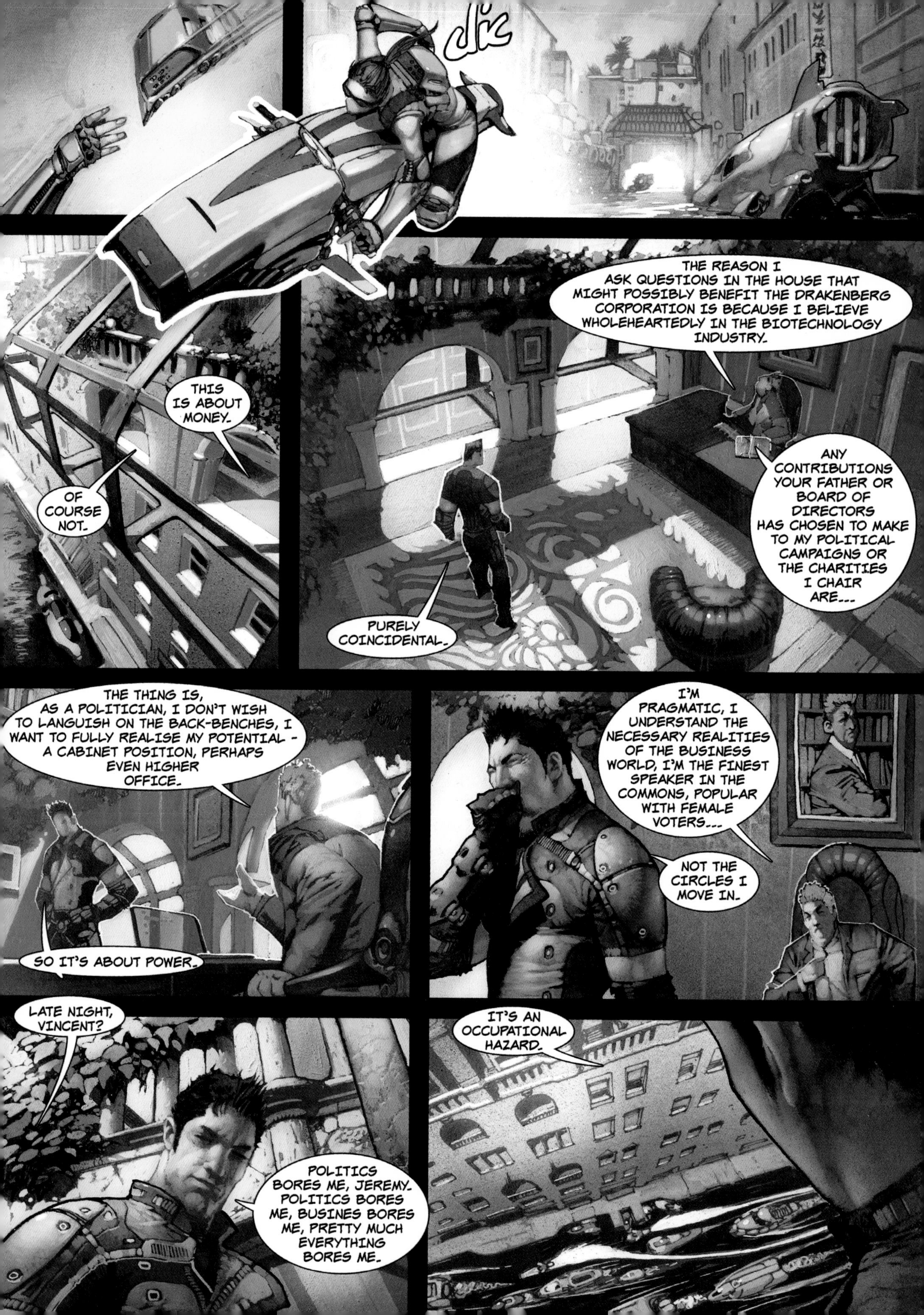
clic
THIS IS ABOUT MONEY.
OF COURSE NOT.
THE REASON I ASK QUESTIONS IN THE HOUSE THAT MIGHT POSSIBLY BENEFIT THE DRAKENBERG CORPORATION IS BECAUSE I BELIEVE WHOLEHEARTEDLY IN THE BIOTECHNOLOGY INDUSTRY.
ANY CONTRIBUTIONS YOUR FATHER OR BOARD OF DIRECTORS HAS CHOSEN TO MAKE TO MY POLITICAL CAMPAIGNS OR THE CHARITIES I CHAIR ARE...
PURELY COINCIDENTAL.
THE THING IS, AS A POLITICIAN, I DON'T WISH TO LANGUISH ON THE BACK-BENCHES, I WANT TO FULLY REALISE MY POTENTIAL - A CABINET POSITION, PERHAPS EVEN HIGHER OFFICE.
SO IT'S ABOUT POWER.
I'M PRAGMATIC, I UNDERSTAND THE NECESSARY REALITIES OF THE BUSINESS WORLD, I'M THE FINEST SPEAKER IN THE COMMONS, POPULAR WITH FEMALE VOTERS...
NOT THE CIRCLES I MOVE IN.
LATE NIGHT, VINCENT?
POLITICS BORES ME, JEREMY. POLITICS BORES ME, BUSINES BORES ME, PRETTY MUCH EVERYTHING BORES ME.
IT'S AN OCCUPATIONAL HAZARD.

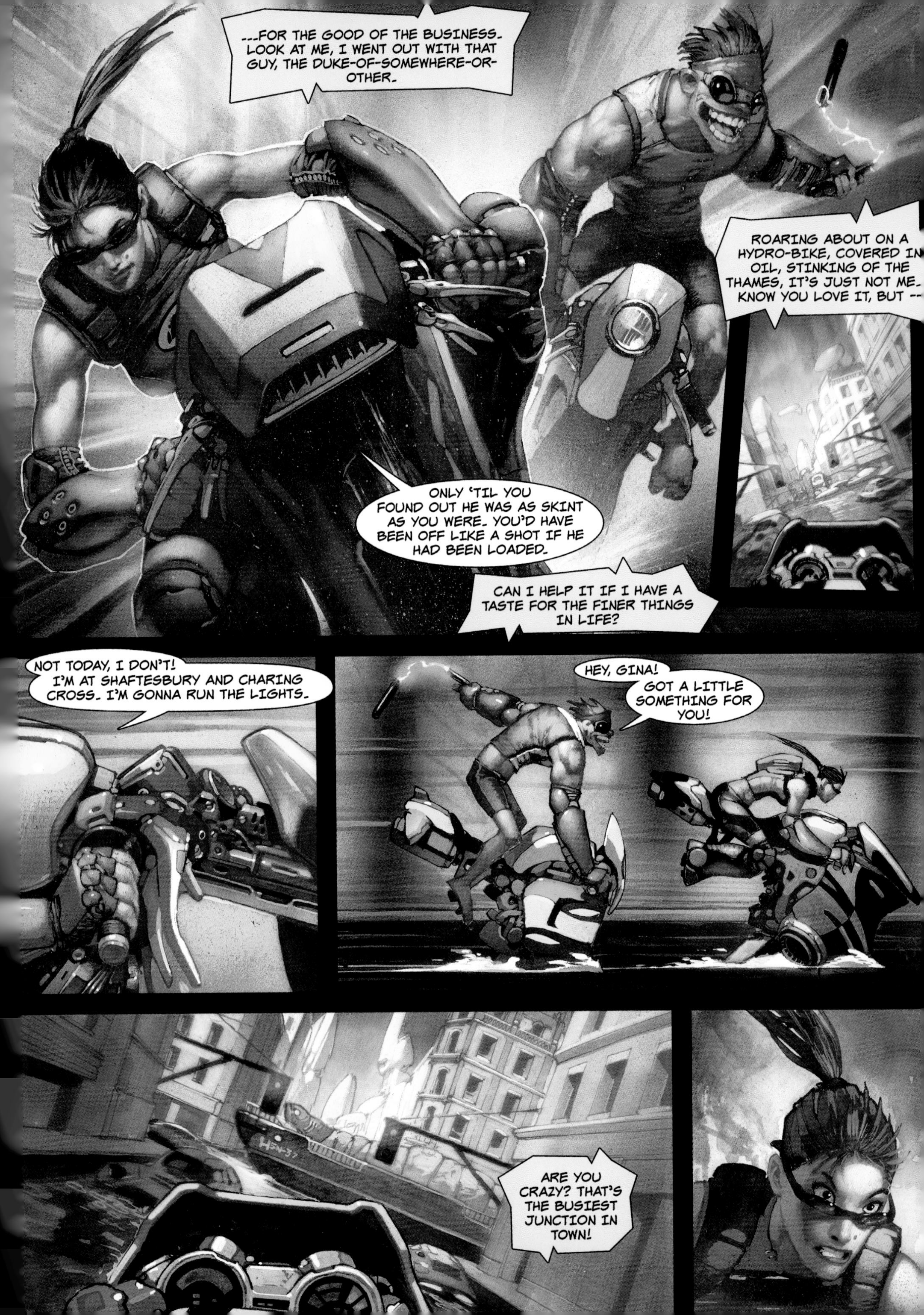
---FOR THE GOOD OF THE BUSINESS. LOOK AT ME, I WENT OUT WITH THAT GUY, THE DUKE-OF-SOMEWHERE-OR-OTHER.
ROARING ABOUT ON A HYDRO-BIKE, COVERED IN OIL, STINKING OF THE THAMES, IT'S JUST NOT ME. KNOW YOU LOVE IT, BUT --
ONLY 'TIL YOU FOUND OUT HE WAS AS SKINT AS YOU WERE. YOU'D HAVE BEEN OFF LIKE A SHOT IF HE HAD BEEN LOADED.
CAN I HELP IT IF I HAVE A TASTE FOR THE FINER THINGS IN LIFE?
NOT TODAY, I DON'T! I'M AT SHAFTESBURY AND CHARING CROSS. I'M GONNA RUN THE LIGHTS.
HEY, GINA! GOT A LITTLE SOMETHING FOR YOU!
ARE YOU CRAZY? THAT'S THE BUSIEST JUNCTION IN TOWN!

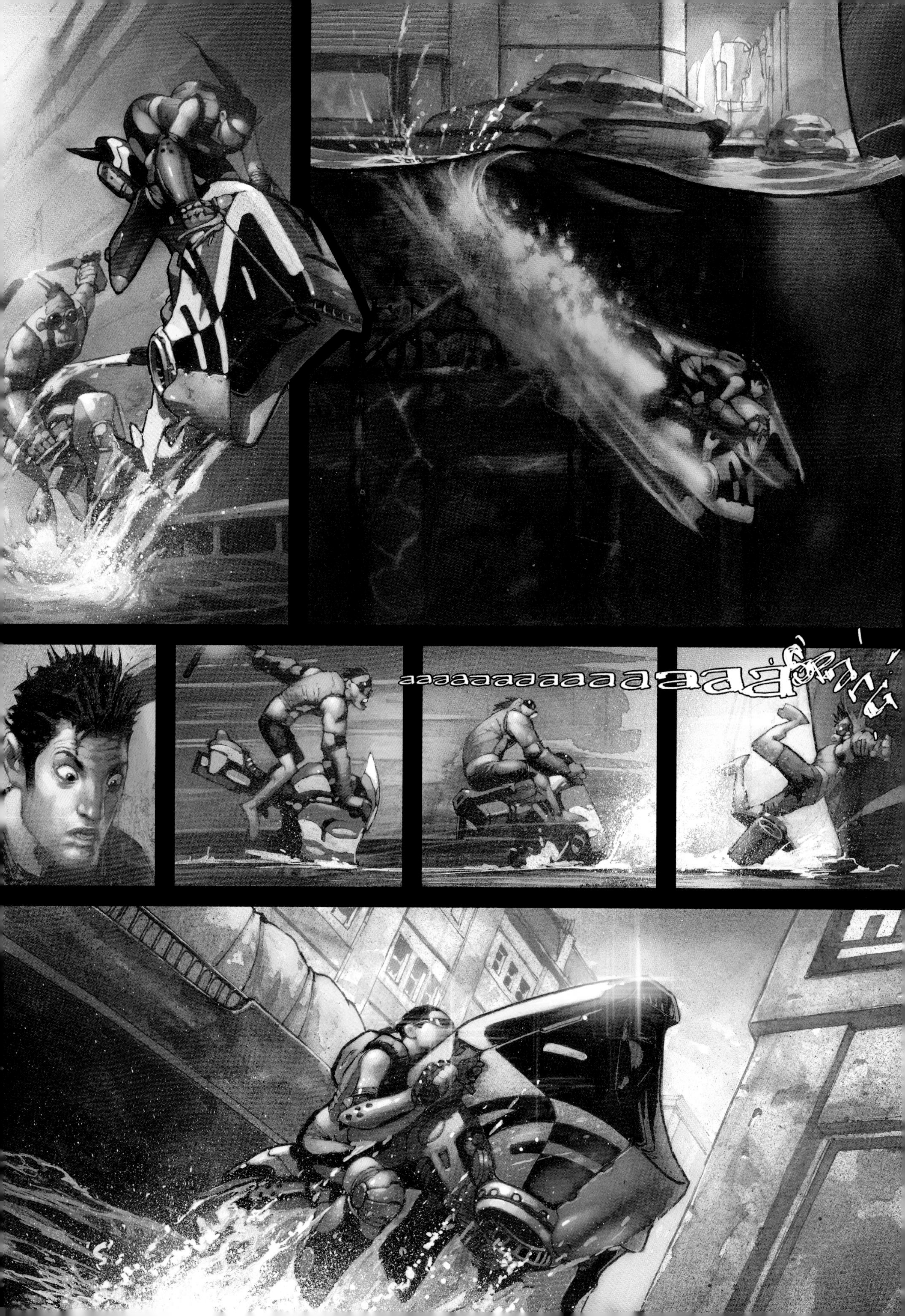
aaaaaaaaaaaaaaa

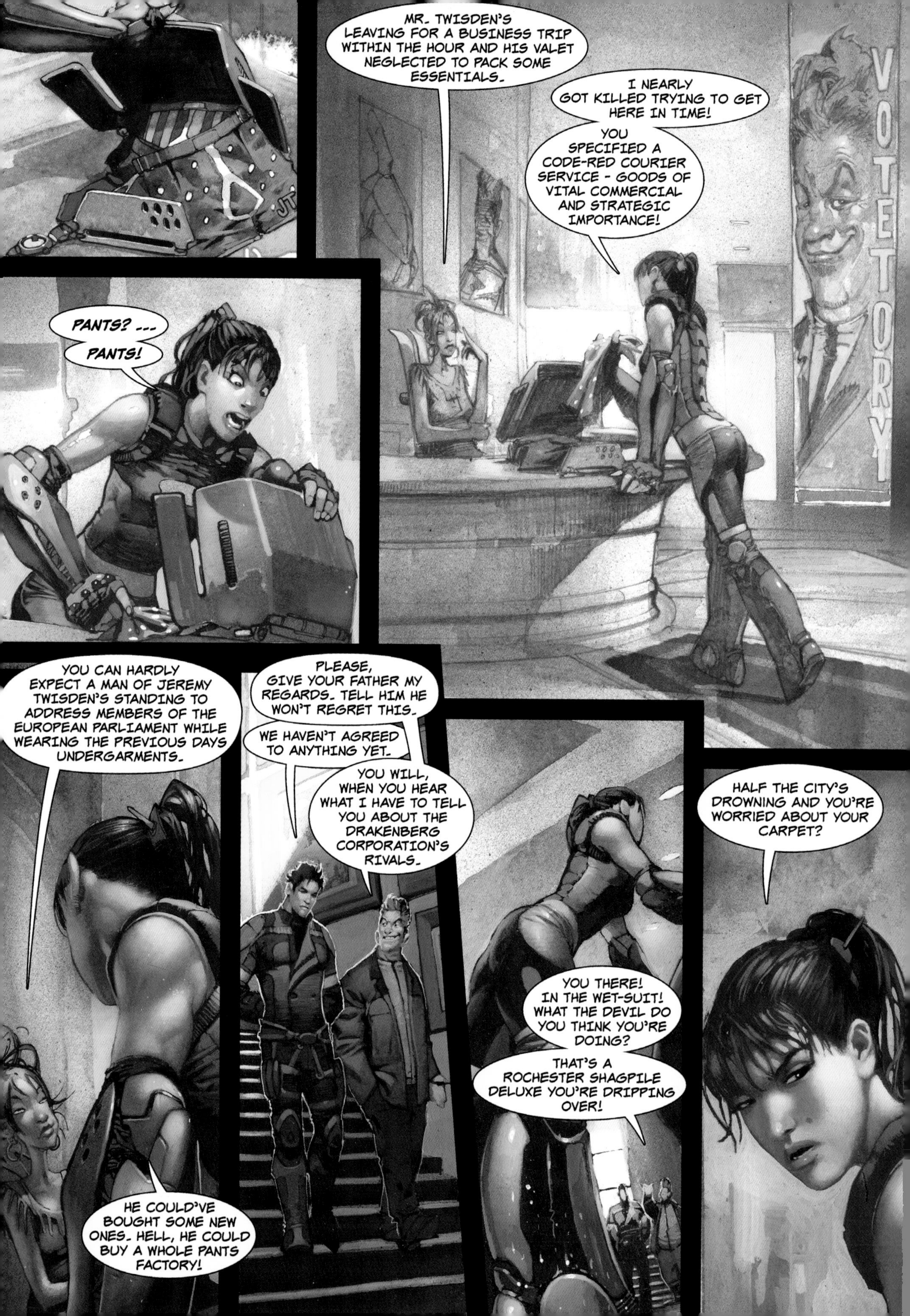
MR. TWISDEN'S LEAVING FOR A BUSINESS TRIP WITHIN THE HOUR AND HIS VALET NEGLECTED TO PACK SOME ESSENTIALS.
I NEARLY GOT KILLED TRYING TO GET HERE IN TIME!
YOU SPECIFIED A CODE-RED COURIER SERVICE - GOODS OF VITAL COMMERCIAL AND STRATEGIC IMPORTANCE!
VOTE TORY
PANTS? ---
PANTS!
YOU CAN HARDLY EXPECT A MAN OF JEREMY TWISDEN'S STANDING TO ADDRESS MEMBERS OF THE EUROPEAN PARLIAMENT WHILE WEARING THE PREVIOUS DAYS UNDERGARMENTS.
HE COULD'VE BOUGHT SOME NEW ONES. HELL, HE COULD BUY A WHOLE PANTS FACTORY!
PLEASE, GIVE YOUR FATHER MY REGARDS. TELL HIM HE WON'T REGRET THIS.
WE HAVEN'T AGREED TO ANYTHING YET.
YOU WILL, WHEN YOU HEAR WHAT I HAVE TO TELL YOU ABOUT THE DRAKENBERG CORPORATION'S RIVALS.
YOU THERE! IN THE WET-SUIT! WHAT THE DEVIL DO YOU THINK YOU'RE DOING?
THAT'S A ROCHESTER SHAGPILE DELUXE YOU'RE DRIPPING OVER!
HALF THE CITY'S DROWNING AND YOU'RE WORRIED ABOUT YOUR CARPET?

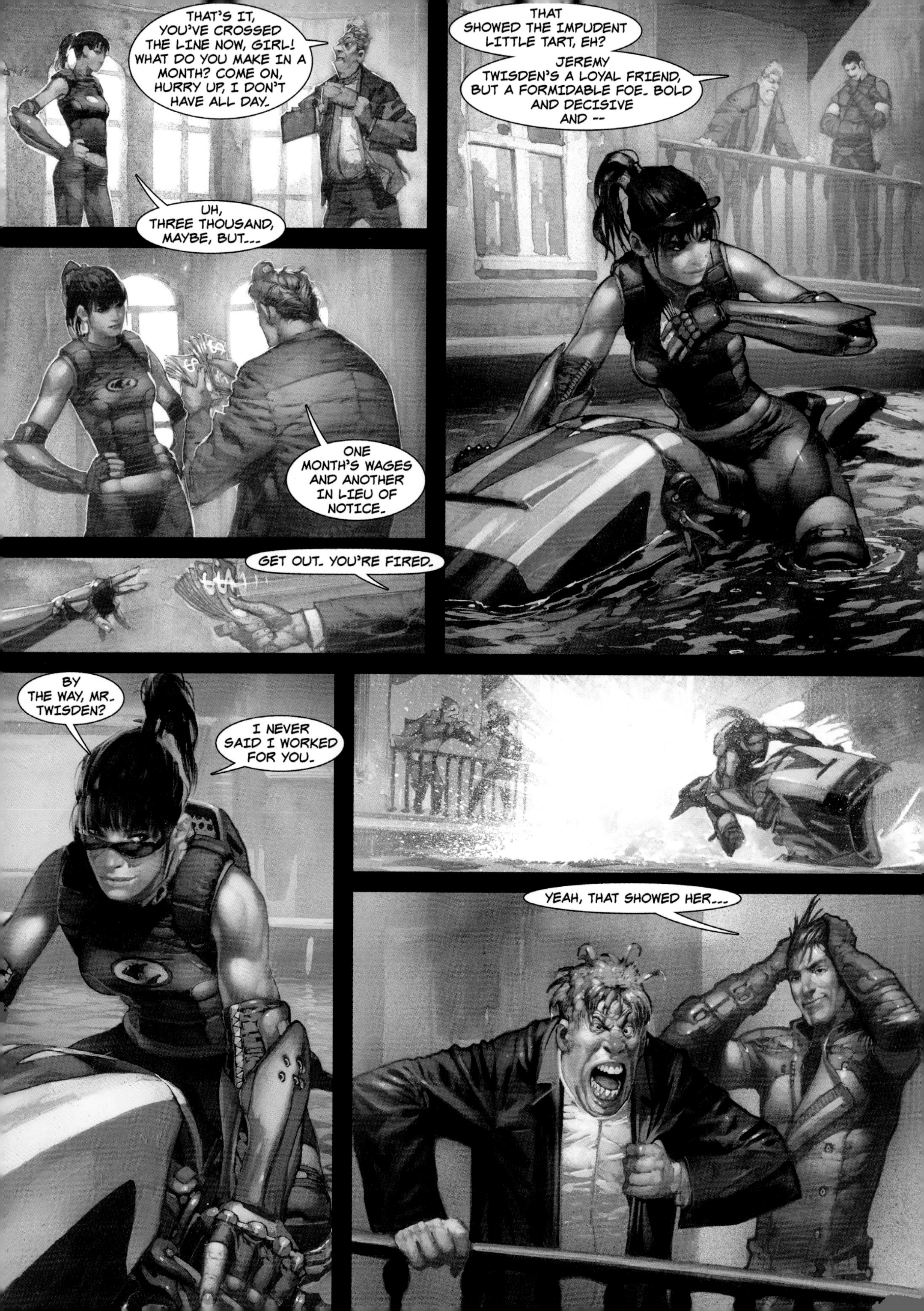
THAT'S IT, YOU'VE CROSSED THE LINE NOW, GIRL! WHAT DO YOU MAKE IN A MONTH? COME ON, HURRY UP, I DON'T HAVE ALL DAY.
UH, THREE THOUSAND, MAYBE, BUT...
ONE MONTH'S WAGES AND ANOTHER IN LIEU OF NOTICE.
GET OUT. YOU'RE FIRED.
THAT SHOWED THE IMPUDENT LITTLE TART, EH?
JEREMY TWISDEN'S A LOYAL FRIEND, BUT A FORMIDABLE FOE. BOLD AND DECISIVE AND --
BY THE WAY, MR. TWISDEN?
I NEVER SAID I WORKED FOR YOU.
YEAH, THAT SHOWED HER...

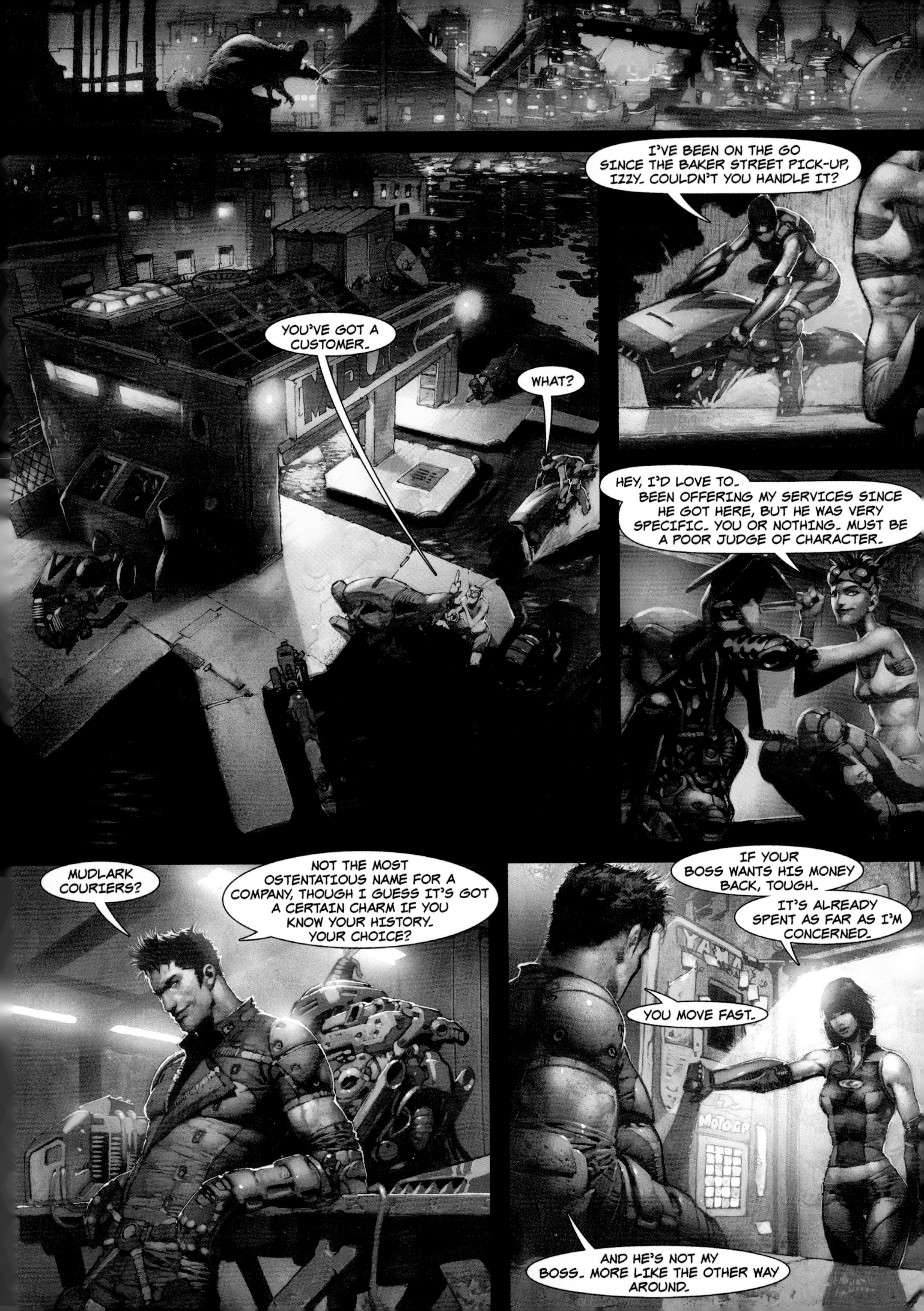
YOU'VE GOT A CUSTOMER.
WHAT?
MUDLARK
I'VE BEEN ON THE GO SINCE THE BAKER STREET PICK-UP, IZZY. COULDN'T YOU HANDLE IT?
HEY, I'D LOVE TO. BEEN OFFERING MY SERVICES SINCE HE GOT HERE, BUT HE WAS VERY SPECIFIC. YOU OR NOTHING. MUST BE A POOR JUDGE OF CHARACTER.
MUDLARK COURIERS?
NOT THE MOST OSTENTATIOUS NAME FOR A COMPANY, THOUGH I GUESS IT'S GOT A CERTAIN CHARM IF YOU KNOW YOUR HISTORY. YOUR CHOICE?
IF YOUR BOSS WANTS HIS MONEY BACK, TOUGH.
IT'S ALREADY SPENT AS FAR AS I'M CONCERNED.
YOU MOVE FAST.
MOTO GP
AND HE'S NOT MY BOSS. MORE LIKE THE OTHER WAY AROUND.

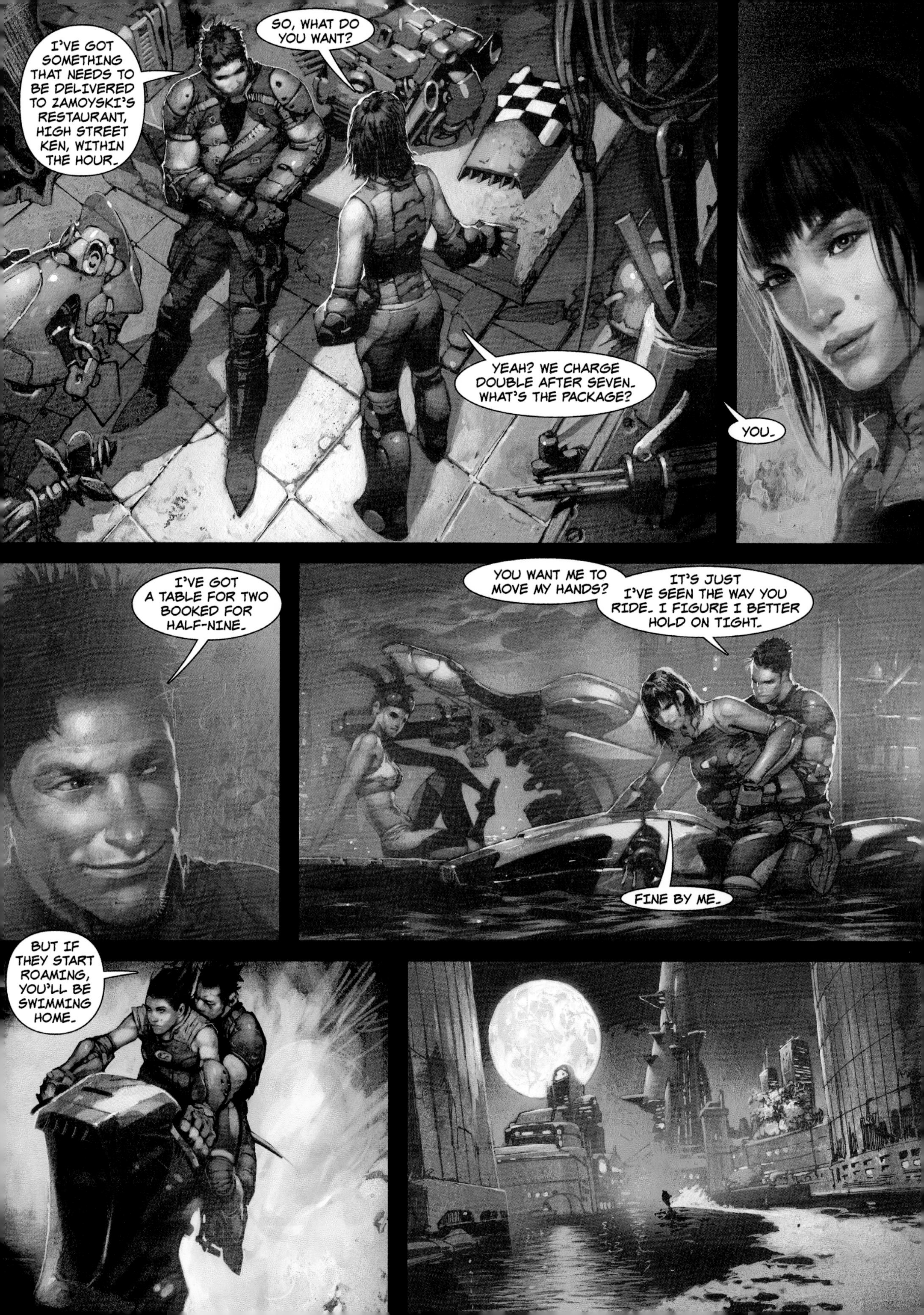
SO, WHAT DO YOU WANT?
I'VE GOT SOMETHING THAT NEEDS TO BE DELIVERED TO ZAMOYSKI'S RESTAURANT, HIGH STREET KEN, WITHIN THE HOUR.
YEAH? WE CHARGE DOUBLE AFTER SEVEN. WHAT'S THE PACKAGE?
YOU.
I'VE GOT A TABLE FOR TWO BOOKED FOR HALF-NINE.
YOU WANT ME TO MOVE MY HANDS?
IT'S JUST I'VE SEEN THE WAY YOU RIDE. I FIGURE I BETTER HOLD ON TIGHT.
FINE BY ME.
BUT IF THEY START ROAMING, YOU'LL BE SWIMMING HOME.

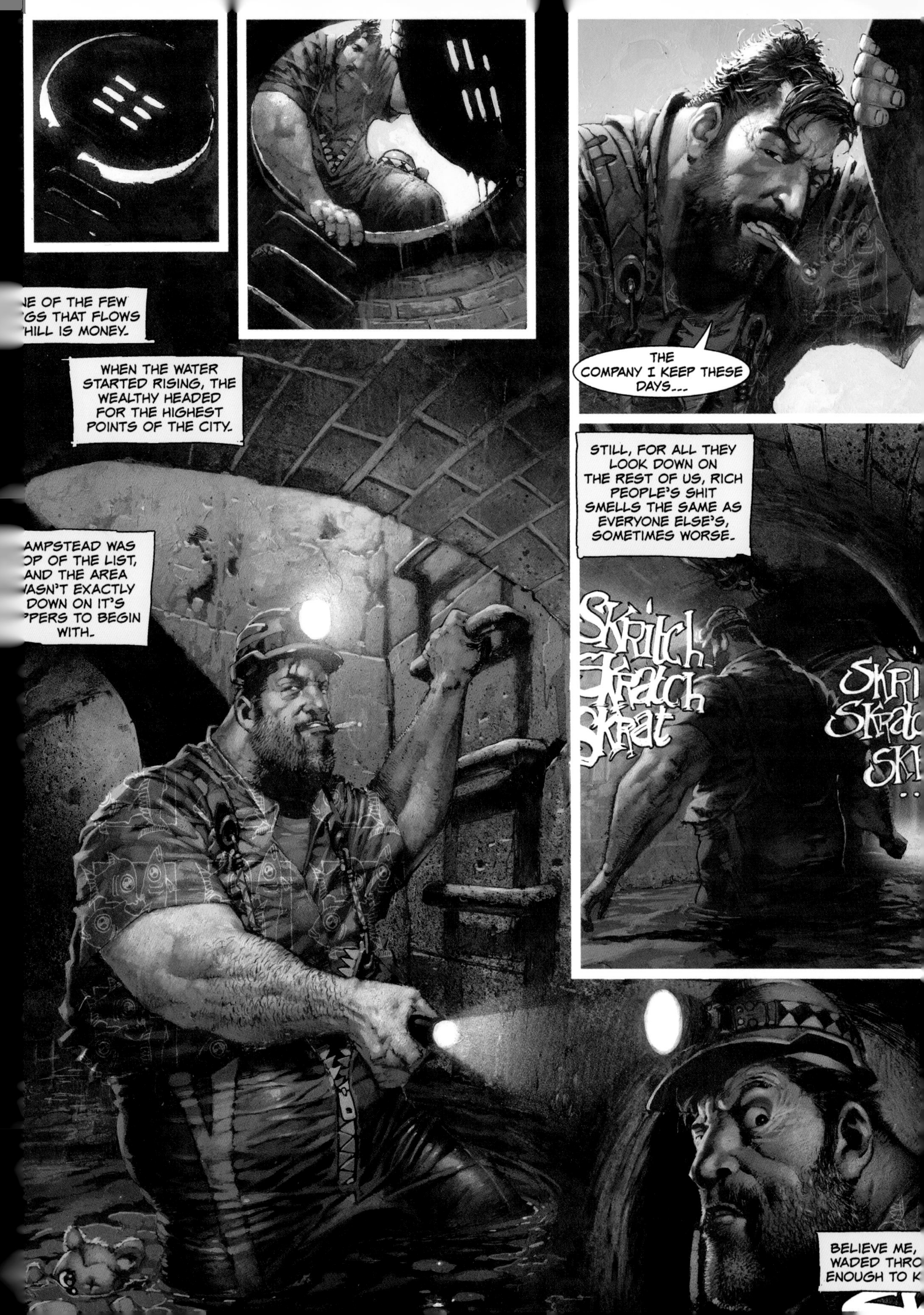
NE OF THE FEW
GS THAT FLOWS
HILL IS MONEY.
WHEN THE WATER STARTED RISING, THE WEALTHY HEADED FOR THE HIGHEST POINTS OF THE CITY.
AMPSTEAD WAS
OP OF THE LIST,
AND THE AREA
ASN'T EXACTLY
DOWN ON IT'S
PPERS TO BEGIN
WITH.
THE COMPANY I KEEP THESE DAYS...
STILL, FOR ALL THEY LOOK DOWN ON THE REST OF US, RICH PEOPLE'S SHIT SMELLS THE SAME AS EVERYONE ELSE'S, SOMETIMES WORSE.
SKRITCH SKRATCH SKRAT
BELIEVE ME,
WADED THRO
ENOUGH TO K

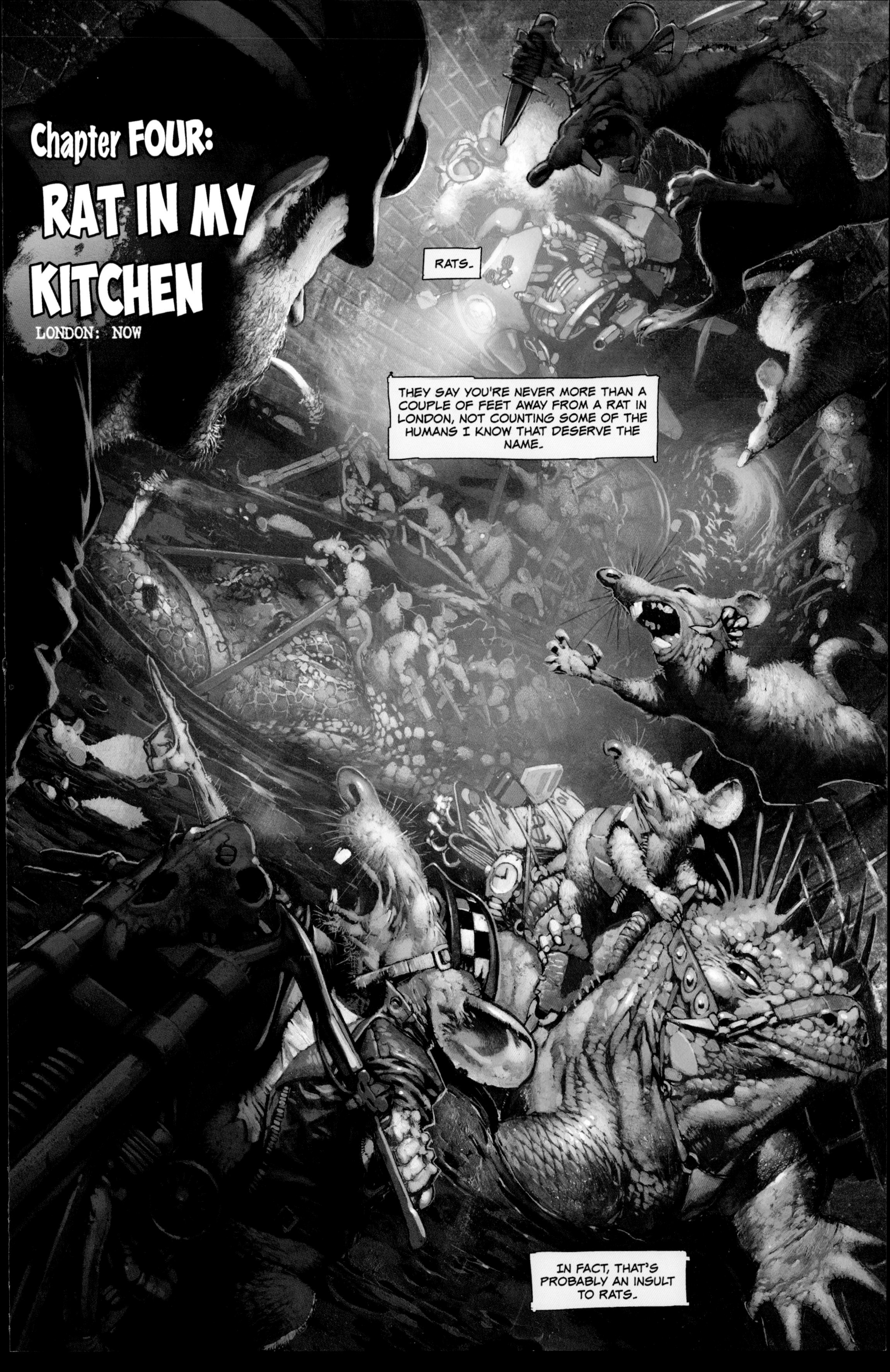
Chapter FOUR:
RAT IN MY KITCHEN
LONDON: NOW
RATS.
THEY SAY YOU'RE NEVER MORE THAN A COUPLE OF FEET AWAY FROM A RAT IN LONDON, NOT COUNTING SOME OF THE HUMANS I KNOW THAT DESERVE THE NAME.
IN FACT, THAT'S PROBABLY AN INSULT TO RATS.

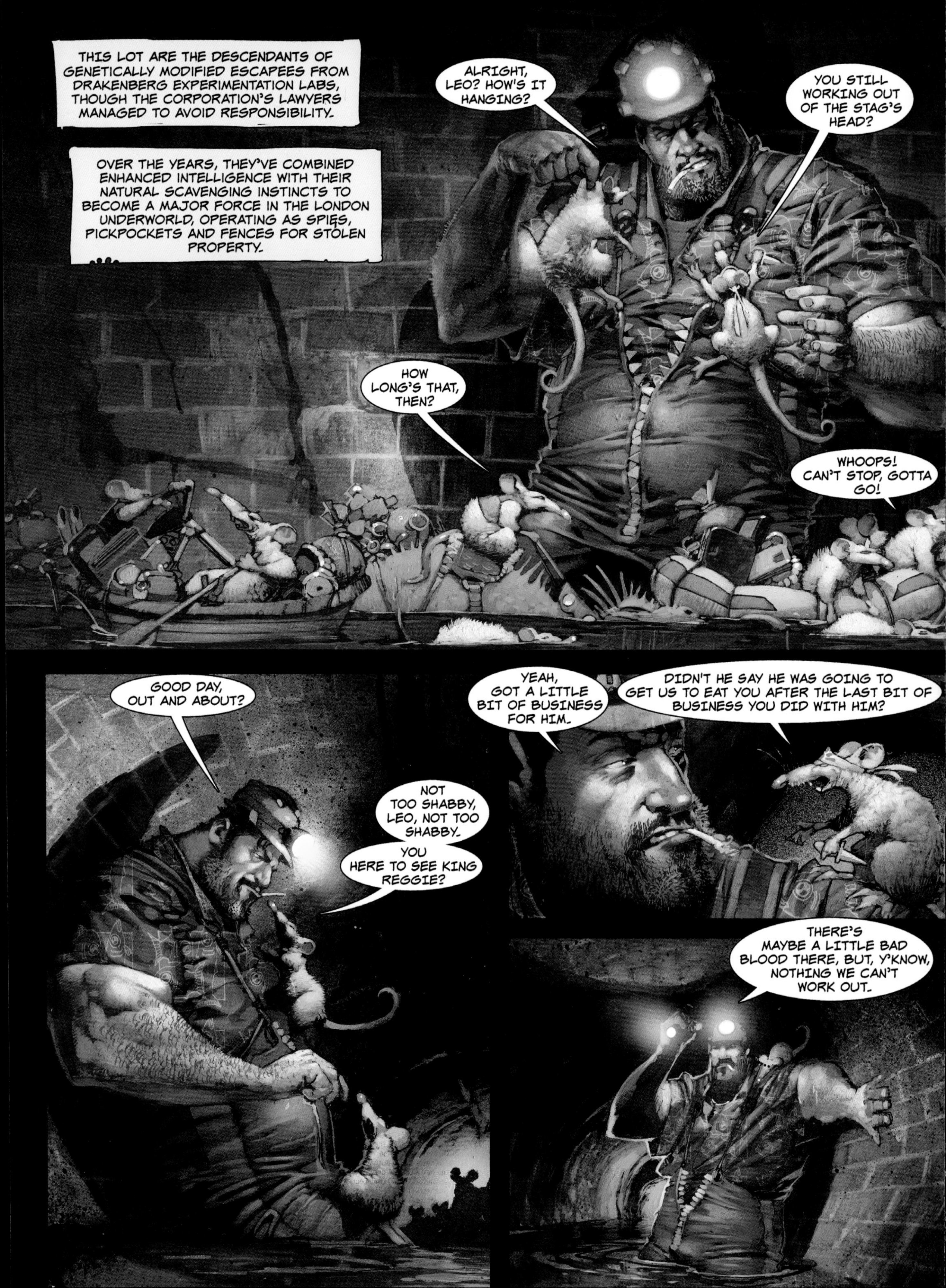
THIS LOT ARE THE DESCENDANTS OF GENETICALLY MODIFIED ESCAPEES FROM DRAKENBERG EXPERIMENTATION LABS, THOUGH THE CORPORATION'S LAWYERS MANAGED TO AVOID RESPONSIBILITY.
OVER THE YEARS, THEY'VE COMBINED ENHANCED INTELLIGENCE WITH THEIR NATURAL SCAVENGING INSTINCTS TO BECOME A MAJOR FORCE IN THE LONDON UNDERWORLD, OPERATING AS SPIES, PICKPOCKETS AND FENCES FOR STOLEN PROPERTY.
ALRIGHT, LEO? HOW'S IT HANGING?
YOU STILL WORKING OUT OF THE STAG'S HEAD?
HOW LONG'S THAT, THEN?
WHOOPS! CAN'T STOP, GOTTA GO!
GOOD DAY, OUT AND ABOUT?
NOT TOO SHABBY, LEO, NOT TOO SHABBY.
YOU HERE TO SEE KING REGGIE?
YEAH, GOT A LITTLE BIT OF BUSINESS FOR HIM.
DIDN'T HE SAY HE WAS GOING TO GET US TO EAT YOU AFTER THE LAST BIT OF BUSINESS YOU DID WITH HIM?
THERE'S MAYBE A LITTLE BAD BLOOD THERE, BUT, Y'KNOW, NOTHING WE CAN'T WORK OUT.

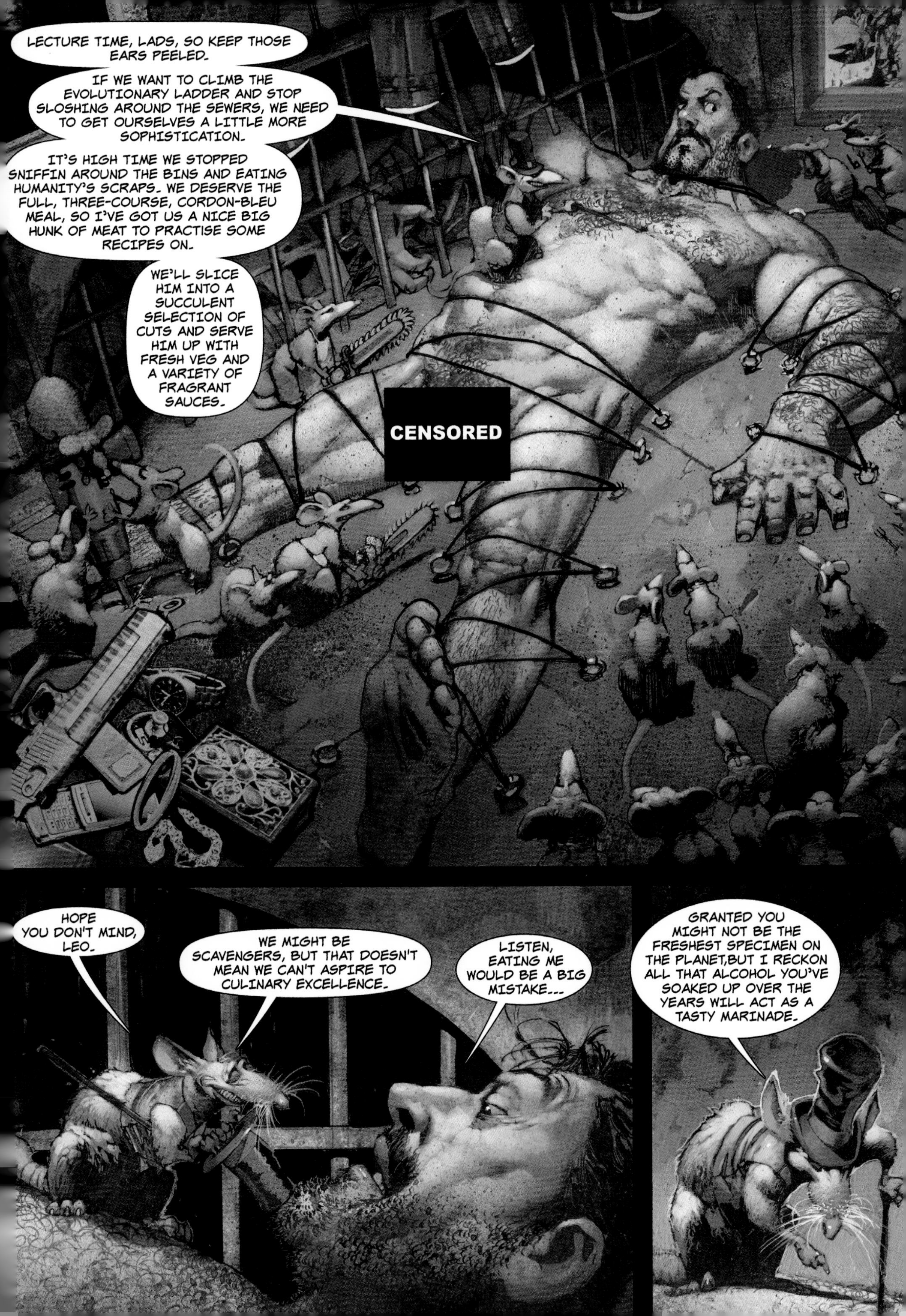
LECTURE TIME, LADS, SO KEEP THOSE EARS PEELED.
IF WE WANT TO CLIMB THE EVOLUTIONARY LADDER AND STOP SLOSHING AROUND THE SEWERS, WE NEED TO GET OURSELVES A LITTLE MORE SOPHISTICATION.
IT'S HIGH TIME WE STOPPED SNIFFIN AROUND THE BINS AND EATING HUMANITY'S SCRAPS. WE DESERVE THE FULL, THREE-COURSE, CORDON-BLEU MEAL, SO I'VE GOT US A NICE BIG HUNK OF MEAT TO PRACTISE SOME RECIPES ON.
WE'LL SLICE HIM INTO A SUCCULENT SELECTION OF CUTS AND SERVE HIM UP WITH FRESH VEG AND A VARIETY OF FRAGRANT SAUCES.
CENSORED
HOPE YOU DON'T MIND, LEO.
WE MIGHT BE SCAVENGERS, BUT THAT DOESN'T MEAN WE CAN'T ASPIRE TO CULINARY EXCELLENCE.
LISTEN, EATING ME WOULD BE A BIG MISTAKE...
GRANTED YOU MIGHT NOT BE THE FRESHEST SPECIMEN ON THE PLANET,BUT I RECKON ALL THAT ALCOHOL YOU'VE SOAKED UP OVER THE YEARS WILL ACT AS A TASTY MARINADE.

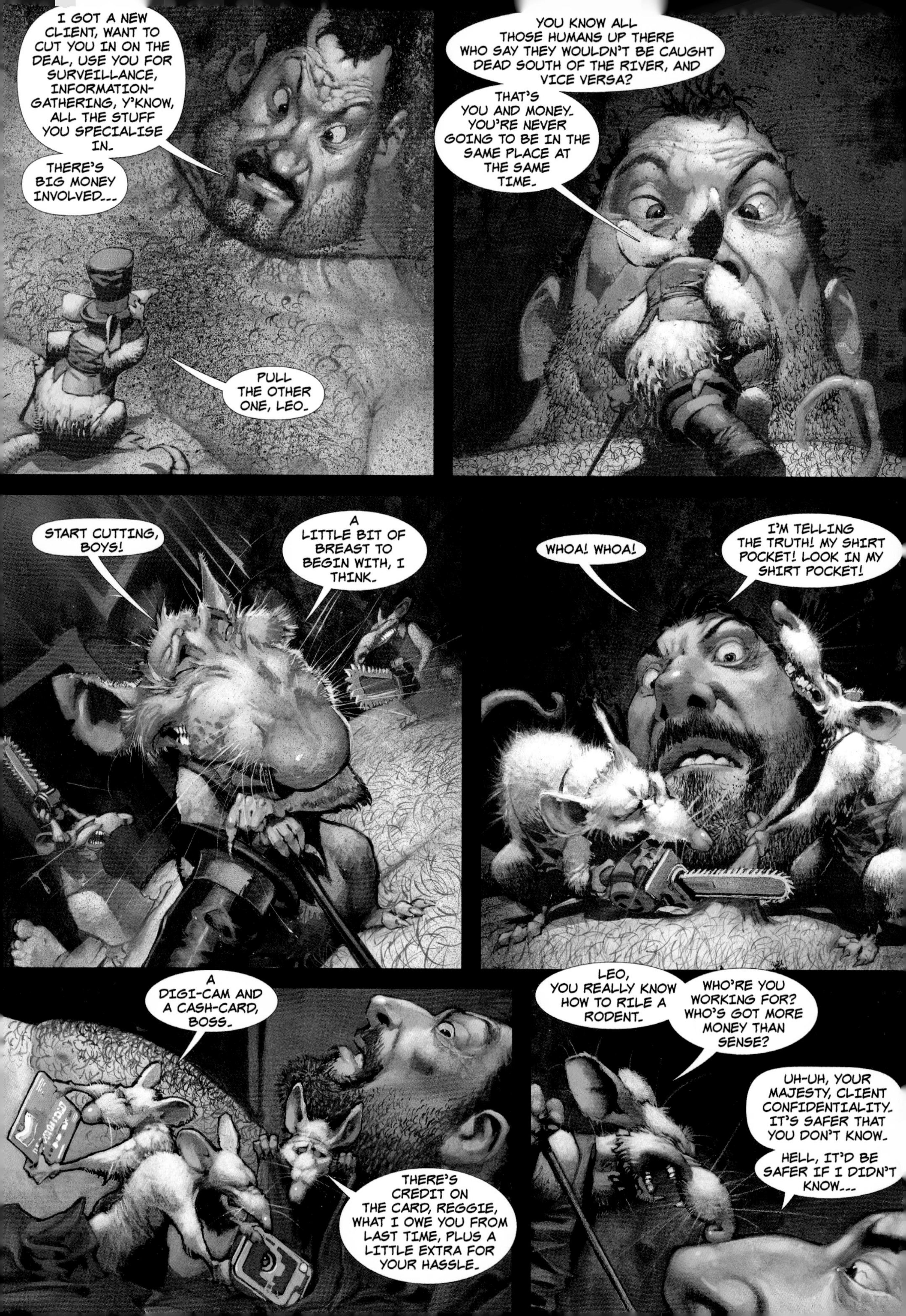
I GOT A NEW CLIENT, WANT TO CUT YOU IN ON THE DEAL, USE YOU FOR SURVEILLANCE, INFORMATION-GATHERING, Y'KNOW, ALL THE STUFF YOU SPECIALISE IN.
THERE'S BIG MONEY INVOLVED...
PULL THE OTHER ONE, LEO.
YOU KNOW ALL THOSE HUMANS UP THERE WHO SAY THEY WOULDN'T BE CAUGHT DEAD SOUTH OF THE RIVER, AND VICE VERSA?
THAT'S YOU AND MONEY. YOU'RE NEVER GOING TO BE IN THE SAME PLACE AT THE SAME TIME.
START CUTTING, BOYS!
A LITTLE BIT OF BREAST TO BEGIN WITH, I THINK.
WHOA! WHOA!
I'M TELLING THE TRUTH! MY SHIRT POCKET! LOOK IN MY SHIRT POCKET!
A DIGI-CAM AND A CASH-CARD, BOSS.
THERE'S CREDIT ON THE CARD, REGGIE, WHAT I OWE YOU FROM LAST TIME, PLUS A LITTLE EXTRA FOR YOUR HASSLE.
LEO, YOU REALLY KNOW HOW TO RILE A RODENT.
WHO'RE YOU WORKING FOR? WHO'S GOT MORE MONEY THAN SENSE?
UH-UH, YOUR MAJESTY, CLIENT CONFIDENTIALITY. IT'S SAFER THAT YOU DON'T KNOW.
HELL, IT'D BE SAFER IF I DIDN'T KNOW...

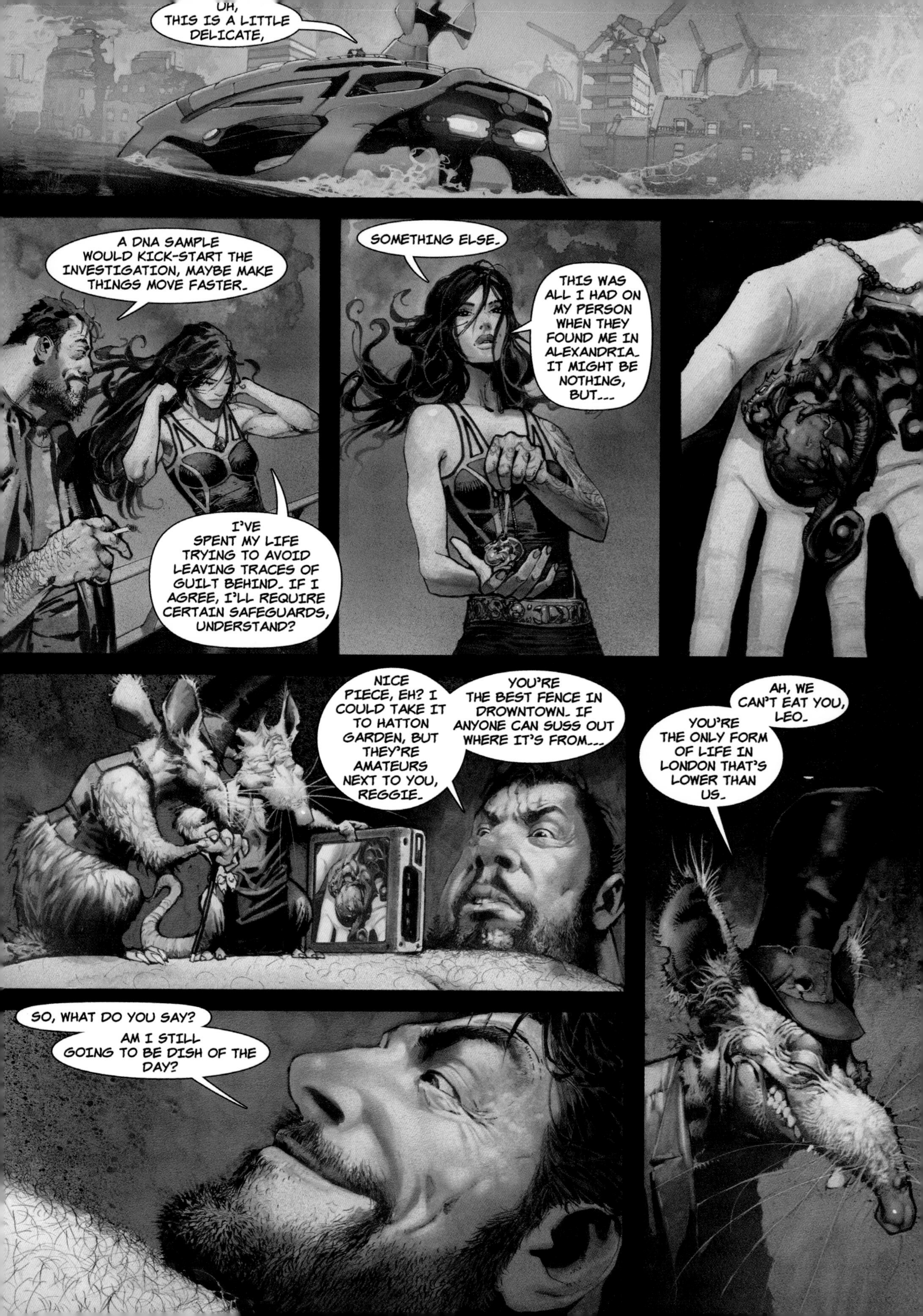
UH, THIS IS A LITTLE DELICATE,
A DNA SAMPLE WOULD KICK-START THE INVESTIGATION, MAYBE MAKE THINGS MOVE FASTER.
I'VE SPENT MY LIFE TRYING TO AVOID LEAVING TRACES OF GUILT BEHIND. IF I AGREE, I'LL REQUIRE CERTAIN SAFEGUARDS, UNDERSTAND?
SOMETHING ELSE.
THIS WAS ALL I HAD ON MY PERSON WHEN THEY FOUND ME IN ALEXANDRIA. IT MIGHT BE NOTHING, BUT...
NICE PIECE, EH? I COULD TAKE IT TO HATTON GARDEN, BUT THEY'RE AMATEURS NEXT TO YOU, REGGIE.
YOU'RE THE BEST FENCE IN DROWNTOWN. IF ANYONE CAN SUSS OUT WHERE IT'S FROM...
AH, WE CAN'T EAT YOU, LEO.
YOU'RE THE ONLY FORM OF LIFE IN LONDON THAT'S LOWER THAN US.
SO, WHAT DO YOU SAY?
AM I STILL GOING TO BE DISH OF THE DAY?

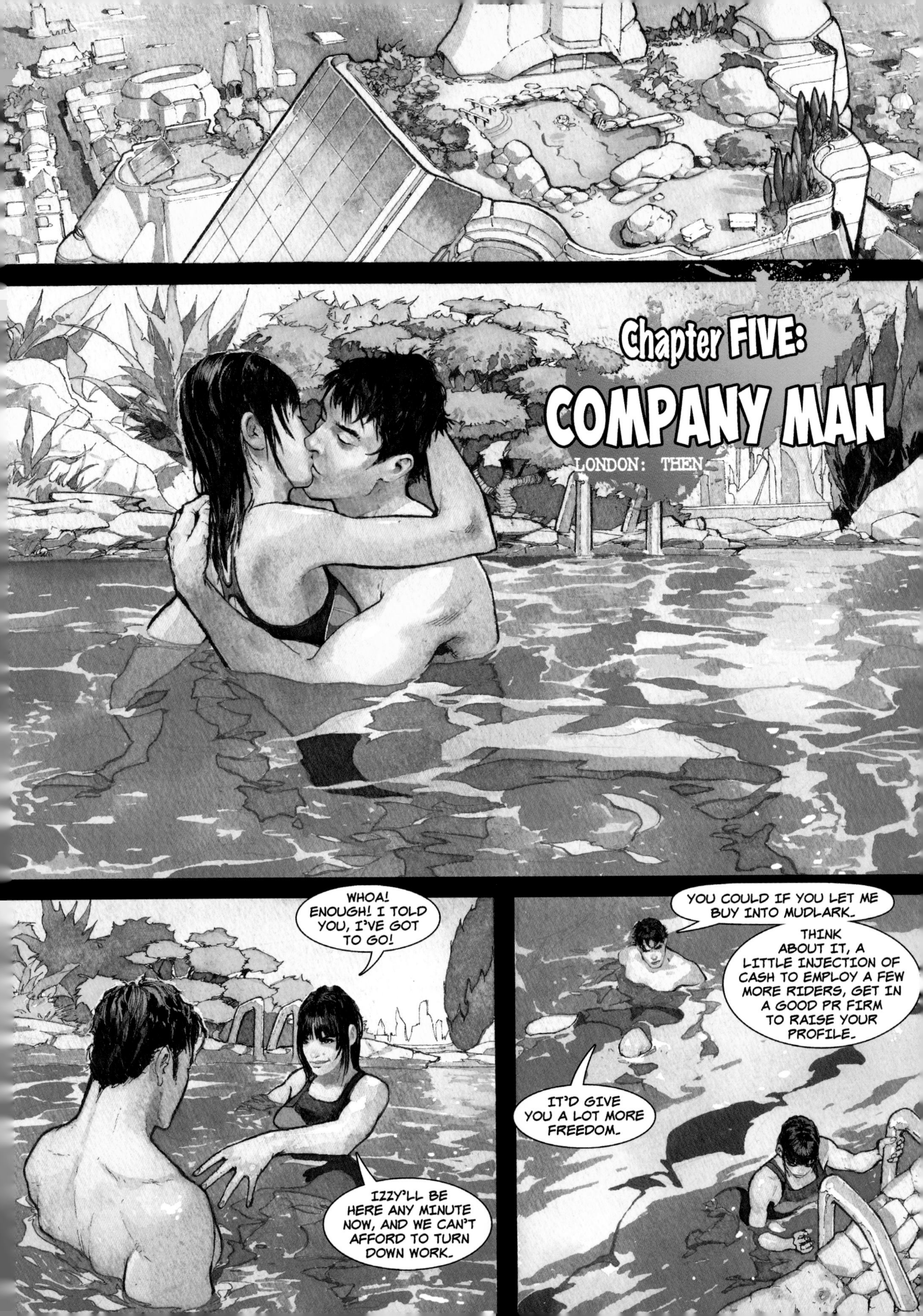
Chapter FIVE:
COMPANY MAN
LONDON: THEN
WHOA! ENOUGH! I TOLD YOU, I'VE GOT TO GO!
IZZY'LL BE HERE ANY MINUTE NOW, AND WE CAN'T AFFORD TO TURN DOWN WORK.
YOU COULD IF YOU LET ME BUY INTO MUDLARK.
THINK ABOUT IT, A LITTLE INJECTION OF CASH TO EMPLOY A FEW MORE RIDERS, GET IN A GOOD PR FIRM TO RAISE YOUR PROFILE.
IT'D GIVE YOU A LOT MORE FREEDOM.

OH, YEAH? FOR WHAT?

TO SPEND MORE TIME WITH ME, WHAT DO YOU THINK?

C'MON, I SWEAR I WOULDN'T INTERFERE. I'D BE A SLEEPING PARTNER.

MORE LIKE A SLEEPING-WITH-YOU PARTNER.

THANKS, BUT WE'RE DOING PRETTY GOOD RIGHT NOW.

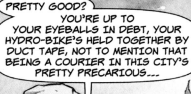

PRETTY GOOD? YOU'RE UP TO YOUR EYEBALLS IN DEBT, YOUR HYDRO-BIKE'S HELD TOGETHER BY DUCT TAPE, NOT TO MENTION THAT BEING A COURIER IN THIS CITY'S PRETTY PRECARIOUS...

YOU CAME OFF YOUR BIKE LAST WEEK AND GOT CAUGHT IN THE UNDERTOW OF AN ADMIRALTY PATROL BOAT. YOU NEARLY DROWNED!

I MEAN, YOU THINK IT'S WORTH IT FOR THE MONEY YOU MAKE?

NOT EVERYTHING'S ABOUT MONEY, VINCENT!

AND MAYBE I LIKE MY WORK! MAYBE I LIKE LIVING DANGEROUSLY!

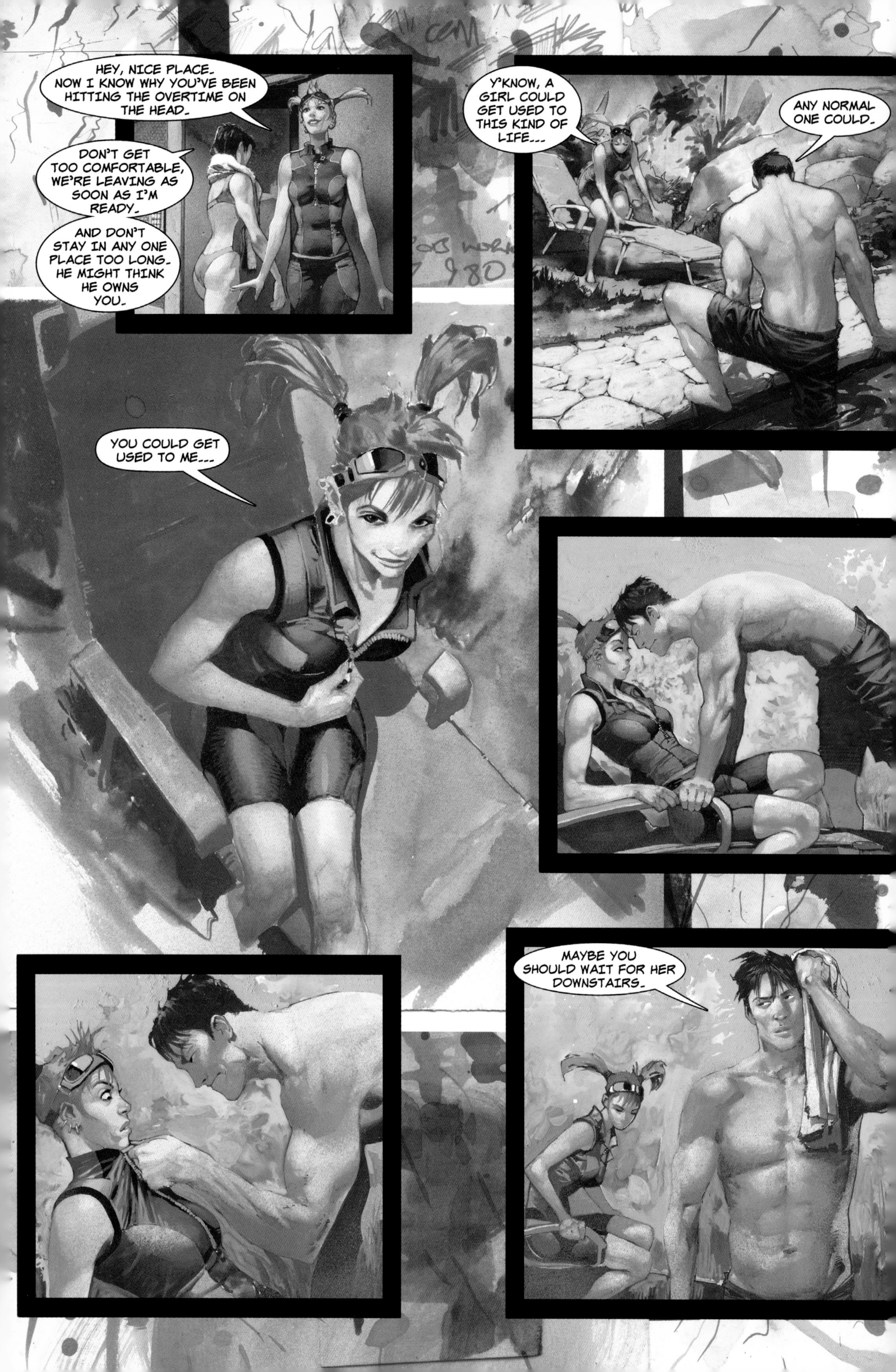
HEY, NICE PLACE. NOW I KNOW WHY YOU'VE BEEN HITTING THE OVERTIME ON THE HEAD.
DON'T GET TOO COMFORTABLE, WE'RE LEAVING AS SOON AS I'M READY.
AND DON'T STAY IN ANY ONE PLACE TOO LONG. HE MIGHT THINK HE OWNS YOU.
Y'KNOW, A GIRL COULD GET USED TO THIS KIND OF LIFE...
ANY NORMAL ONE COULD.
YOU COULD GET USED TO ME...
MAYBE YOU SHOULD WAIT FOR HER DOWNSTAIRS.

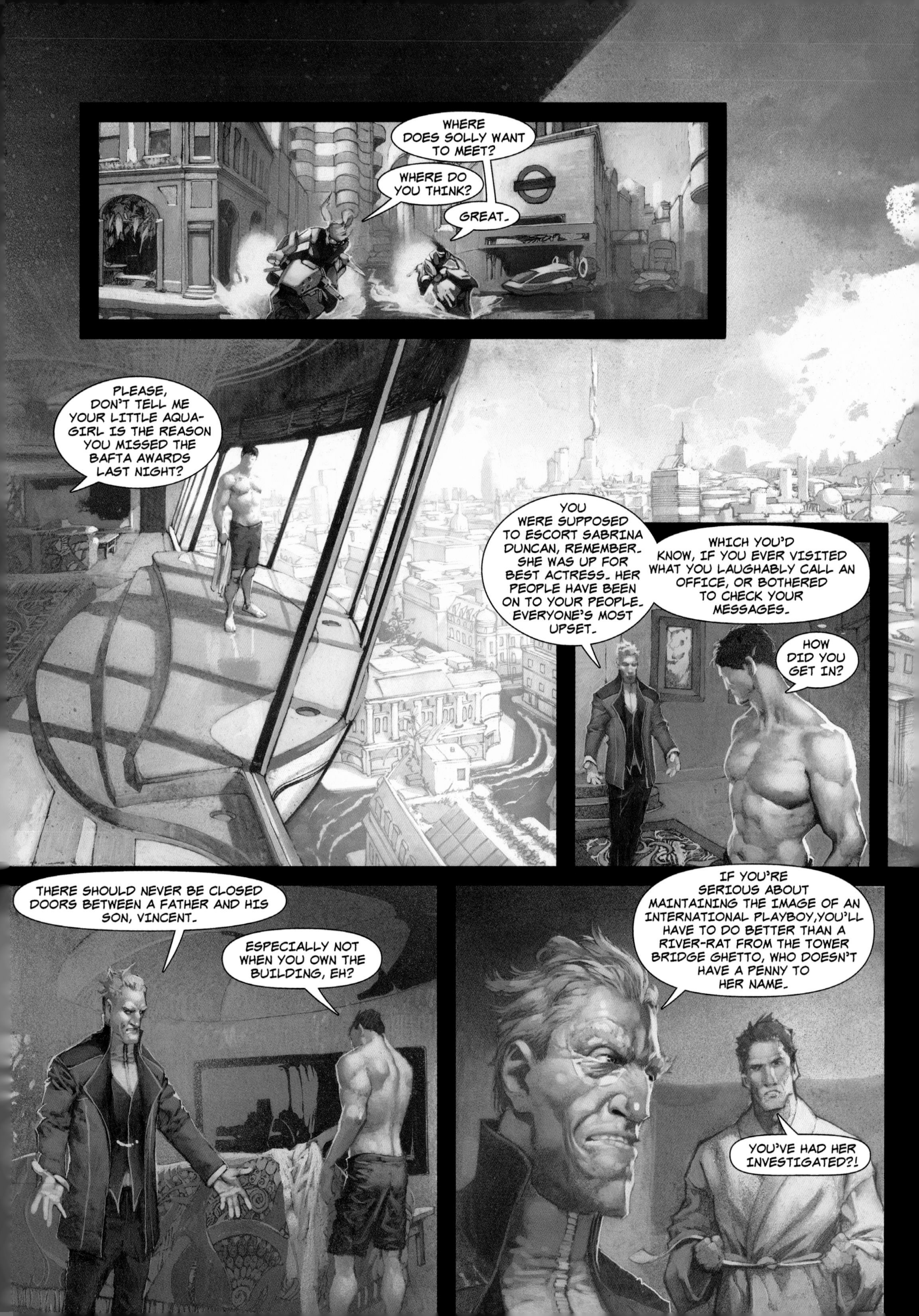
WHERE DOES SOLLY WANT TO MEET?
WHERE DO YOU THINK?
GREAT.
PLEASE, DON'T TELL ME YOUR LITTLE AQUA-GIRL IS THE REASON YOU MISSED THE BAFTA AWARDS LAST NIGHT?
YOU WERE SUPPOSED TO ESCORT SABRINA DUNCAN, REMEMBER. SHE WAS UP FOR BEST ACTRESS. HER PEOPLE HAVE BEEN ON TO YOUR PEOPLE. EVERYONE'S MOST UPSET.
WHICH YOU'D KNOW, IF YOU EVER VISITED WHAT YOU LAUGHABLY CALL AN OFFICE, OR BOTHERED TO CHECK YOUR MESSAGES.
HOW DID YOU GET IN?
THERE SHOULD NEVER BE CLOSED DOORS BETWEEN A FATHER AND HIS SON, VINCENT.
ESPECIALLY NOT WHEN YOU OWN THE BUILDING, EH?
IF YOU'RE SERIOUS ABOUT MAINTAINING THE IMAGE OF AN INTERNATIONAL PLAYBOY,YOU'LL HAVE TO DO BETTER THAN A RIVER-RAT FROM THE TOWER BRIDGE GHETTO, WHO DOESN'T HAVE A PENNY TO HER NAME.
YOU'VE HAD HER INVESTIGATED?!

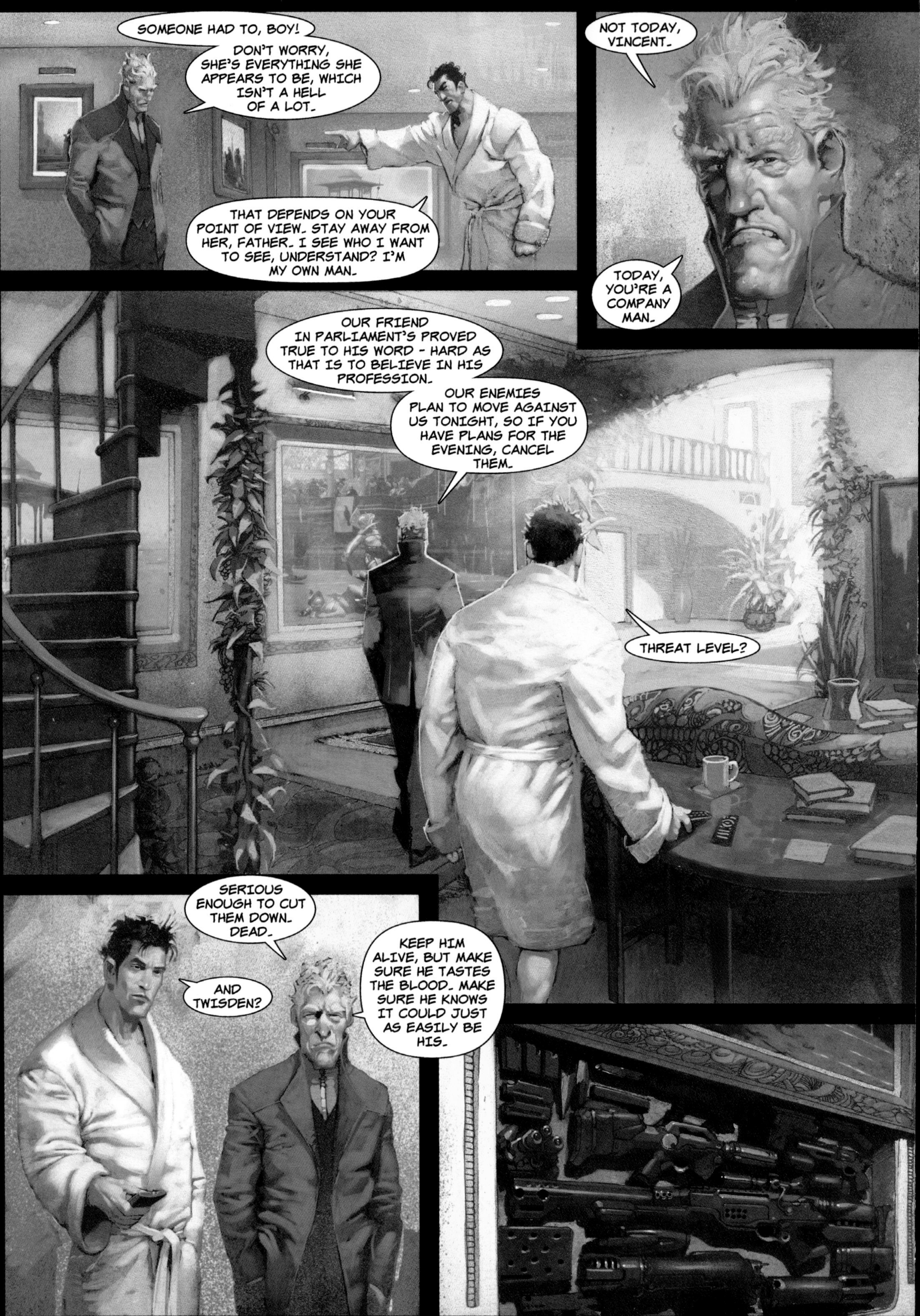
SOMEONE HAD TO, BOY!
DON'T WORRY, SHE'S EVERYTHING SHE APPEARS TO BE, WHICH ISN'T A HELL OF A LOT.
THAT DEPENDS ON YOUR POINT OF VIEW. STAY AWAY FROM HER, FATHER. I SEE WHO I WANT TO SEE, UNDERSTAND? I'M MY OWN MAN.
NOT TODAY, VINCENT.
TODAY, YOU'RE A COMPANY MAN.
OUR FRIEND IN PARLIAMENT'S PROVED TRUE TO HIS WORD - HARD AS THAT IS TO BELIEVE IN HIS PROFESSION.
OUR ENEMIES PLAN TO MOVE AGAINST US TONIGHT, SO IF YOU HAVE PLANS FOR THE EVENING, CANCEL THEM.
THREAT LEVEL?
SERIOUS ENOUGH TO CUT THEM DOWN. DEAD.
AND TWISDEN?
KEEP HIM ALIVE, BUT MAKE SURE HE TASTES THE BLOOD. MAKE SURE HE KNOWS IT COULD JUST AS EASILY BE HIS.

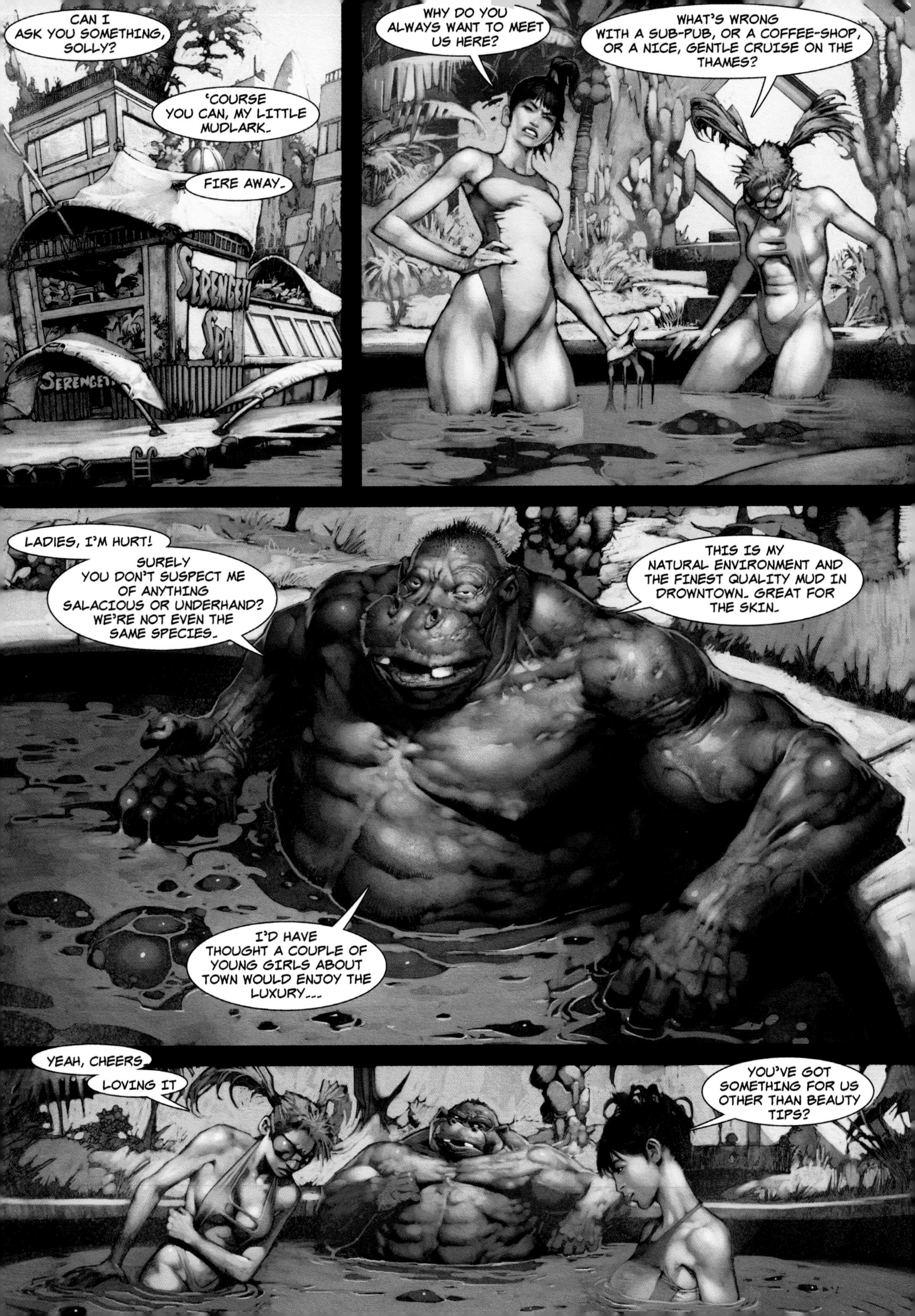
CAN I ASK YOU SOMETHING, SOLLY?
'COURSE YOU CAN, MY LITTLE MUDLARK.
FIRE AWAY.
SERENGETI SPA
SERENGETI
WHY DO YOU ALWAYS WANT TO MEET US HERE?
WHAT'S WRONG WITH A SUB-PUB, OR A COFFEE-SHOP, OR A NICE, GENTLE CRUISE ON THE THAMES?
LADIES, I'M HURT!
SURELY YOU DON'T SUSPECT ME OF ANYTHING SALACIOUS OR UNDERHAND? WE'RE NOT EVEN THE SAME SPECIES.
THIS IS MY NATURAL ENVIRONMENT AND THE FINEST QUALITY MUD IN DROWNTOWN. GREAT FOR THE SKIN.
I'D HAVE THOUGHT A COUPLE OF YOUNG GIRLS ABOUT TOWN WOULD ENJOY THE LUXURY...
YEAH, CHEERS.
LOVING IT
YOU'VE GOT SOMETHING FOR US OTHER THAN BEAUTY TIPS?

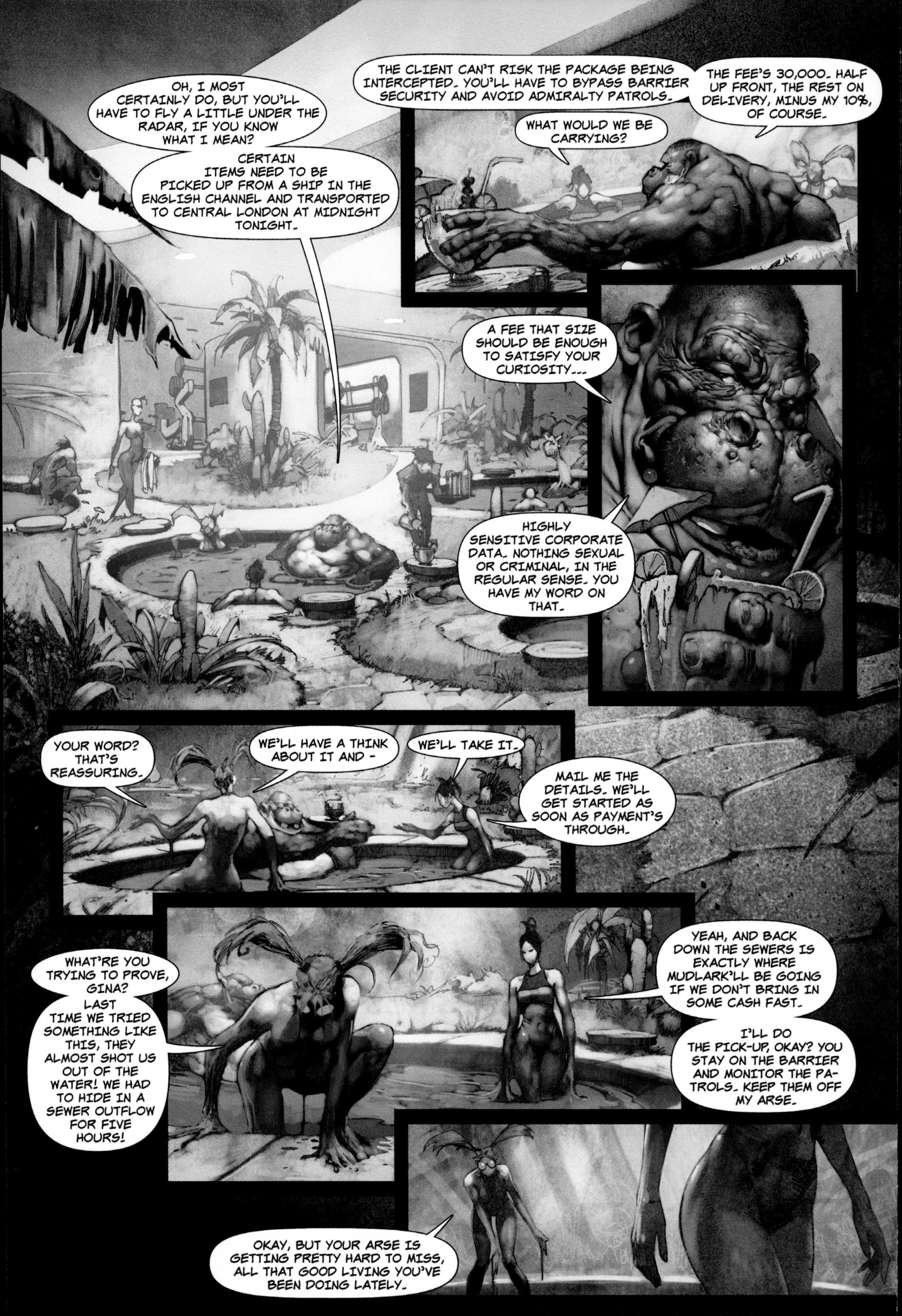
OH, I MOST CERTAINLY DO, BUT YOU'LL HAVE TO FLY A LITTLE UNDER THE RADAR, IF YOU KNOW WHAT I MEAN?
CERTAIN ITEMS NEED TO BE PICKED UP FROM A SHIP IN THE ENGLISH CHANNEL AND TRANSPORTED TO CENTRAL LONDON AT MIDNIGHT TONIGHT.
THE CLIENT CAN'T RISK THE PACKAGE BEING INTERCEPTED. YOU'LL HAVE TO BYPASS BARRIER SECURITY AND AVOID ADMIRALTY PATROLS.
THE FEE'S 30,000. HALF UP FRONT, THE REST ON DELIVERY, MINUS MY 10%, OF COURSE.
WHAT WOULD WE BE CARRYING?
A FEE THAT SIZE SHOULD BE ENOUGH TO SATISFY YOUR CURIOSITY...
HIGHLY SENSITIVE CORPORATE DATA. NOTHING SEXUAL OR CRIMINAL, IN THE REGULAR SENSE. YOU HAVE MY WORD ON THAT.
YOUR WORD? THAT'S REASSURING.
WE'LL HAVE A THINK ABOUT IT AND -
WE'LL TAKE IT.
MAIL ME THE DETAILS. WE'LL GET STARTED AS SOON AS PAYMENT'S THROUGH.
WHAT'RE YOU TRYING TO PROVE, GINA?
LAST TIME WE TRIED SOMETHING LIKE THIS, THEY ALMOST SHOT US OUT OF THE WATER! WE HAD TO HIDE IN A SEWER OUTFLOW FOR FIVE HOURS!
YEAH, AND BACK DOWN THE SEWERS IS EXACTLY WHERE MUDLARK'LL BE GOING IF WE DON'T BRING IN SOME CASH FAST.
I'LL DO THE PICK-UP, OKAY? YOU STAY ON THE BARRIER AND MONITOR THE PATROLS. KEEP THEM OFF MY ARSE.
OKAY, BUT YOUR ARSE IS GETTING PRETTY HARD TO MISS, ALL THAT GOOD LIVING YOU'VE BEEN DOING LATELY.

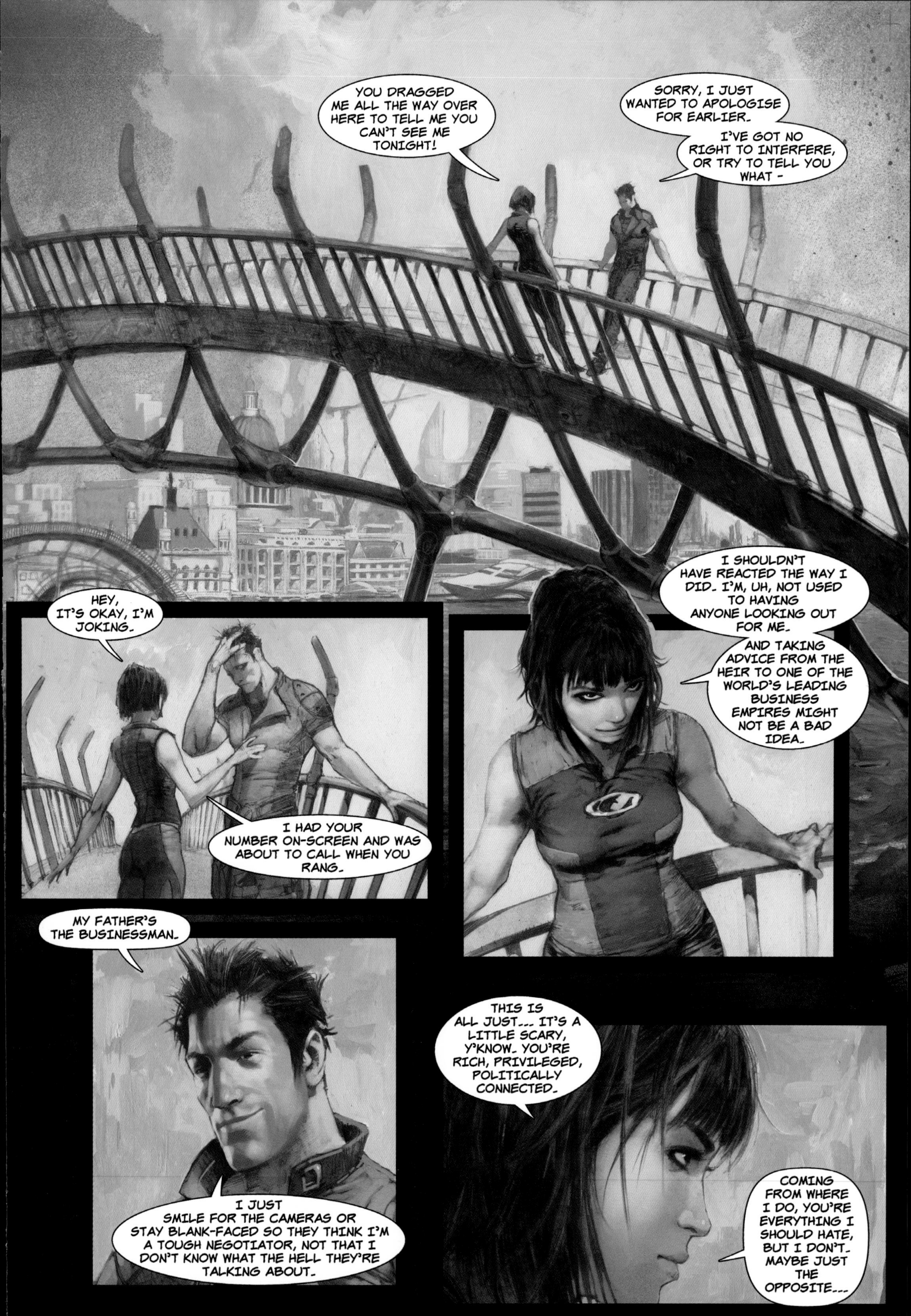
YOU DRAGGED ME ALL THE WAY OVER HERE TO TELL ME YOU CAN'T SEE ME TONIGHT!
SORRY, I JUST WANTED TO APOLOGISE FOR EARLIER.
I'VE GOT NO RIGHT TO INTERFERE, OR TRY TO TELL YOU WHAT -
HEY, IT'S OKAY, I'M JOKING.
I HAD YOUR NUMBER ON-SCREEN AND WAS ABOUT TO CALL WHEN YOU RANG.
I SHOULDN'T HAVE REACTED THE WAY I DID. I'M, UH, NOT USED TO HAVING ANYONE LOOKING OUT FOR ME.
AND TAKING ADVICE FROM THE HEIR TO ONE OF THE WORLD'S LEADING BUSINESS EMPIRES MIGHT NOT BE A BAD IDEA.
MY FATHER'S THE BUSINESSMAN.
I JUST SMILE FOR THE CAMERAS OR STAY BLANK-FACED SO THEY THINK I'M A TOUGH NEGOTIATOR, NOT THAT I DON'T KNOW WHAT THE HELL THEY'RE TALKING ABOUT.
THIS IS ALL JUST... IT'S A LITTLE SCARY, Y'KNOW. YOU'RE RICH, PRIVILEGED, POLITICALLY CONNECTED.
COMING FROM WHERE I DO, YOU'RE EVERYTHING I SHOULD HATE, BUT I DON'T. MAYBE JUST THE OPPOSITE...

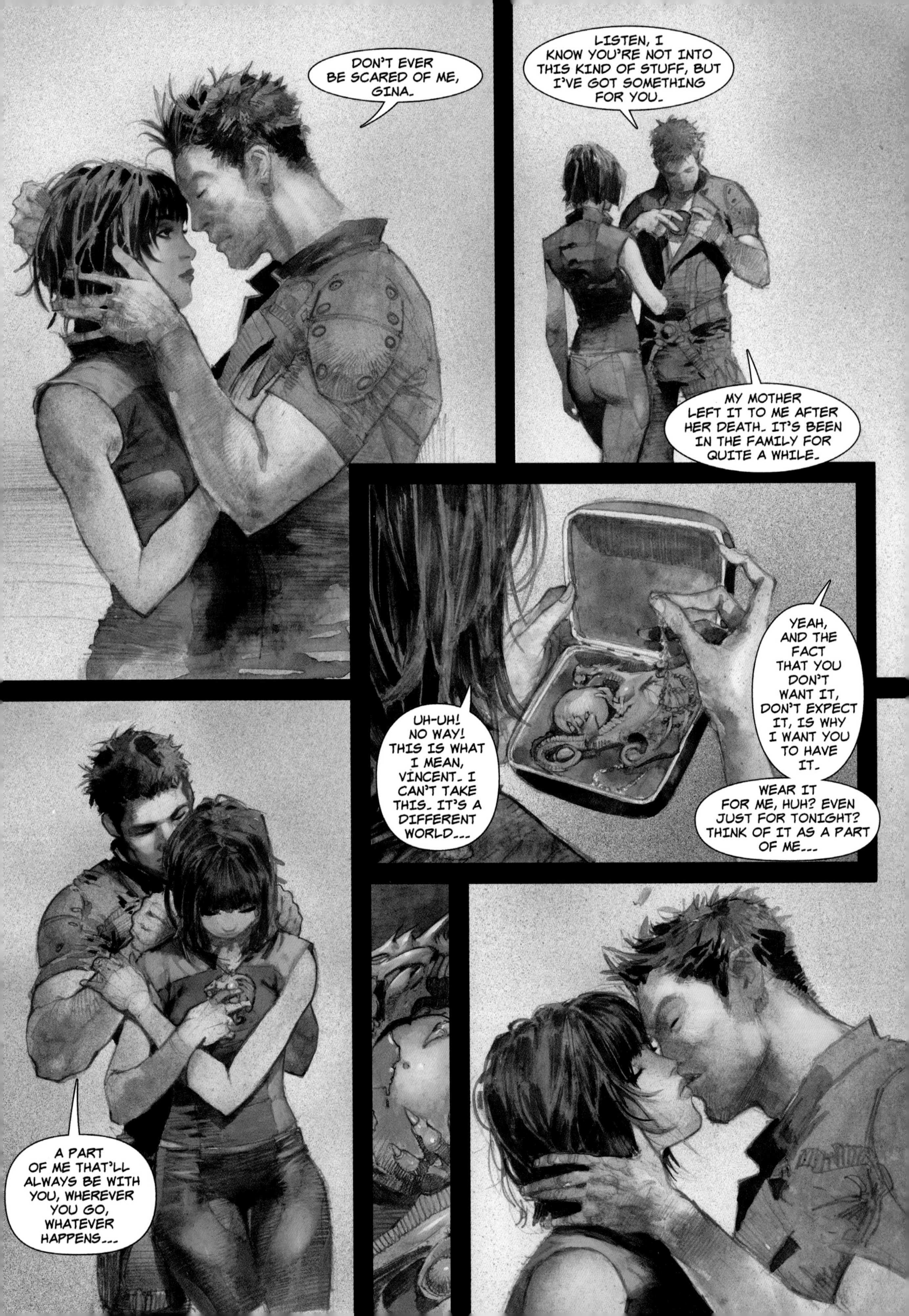
DON'T EVER BE SCARED OF ME, GINA.
LISTEN, I KNOW YOU'RE NOT INTO THIS KIND OF STUFF, BUT I'VE GOT SOMETHING FOR YOU.
MY MOTHER LEFT IT TO ME AFTER HER DEATH. IT'S BEEN IN THE FAMILY FOR QUITE A WHILE.
UH-UH! NO WAY! THIS IS WHAT I MEAN, VINCENT. I CAN'T TAKE THIS. IT'S A DIFFERENT WORLD...
YEAH, AND THE FACT THAT YOU DON'T WANT IT, DON'T EXPECT IT, IS WHY I WANT YOU TO HAVE IT.
WEAR IT FOR ME, HUH? EVEN JUST FOR TONIGHT? THINK OF IT AS A PART OF ME...
A PART OF ME THAT'LL ALWAYS BE WITH YOU, WHEREVER YOU GO, WHATEVER HAPPENS...

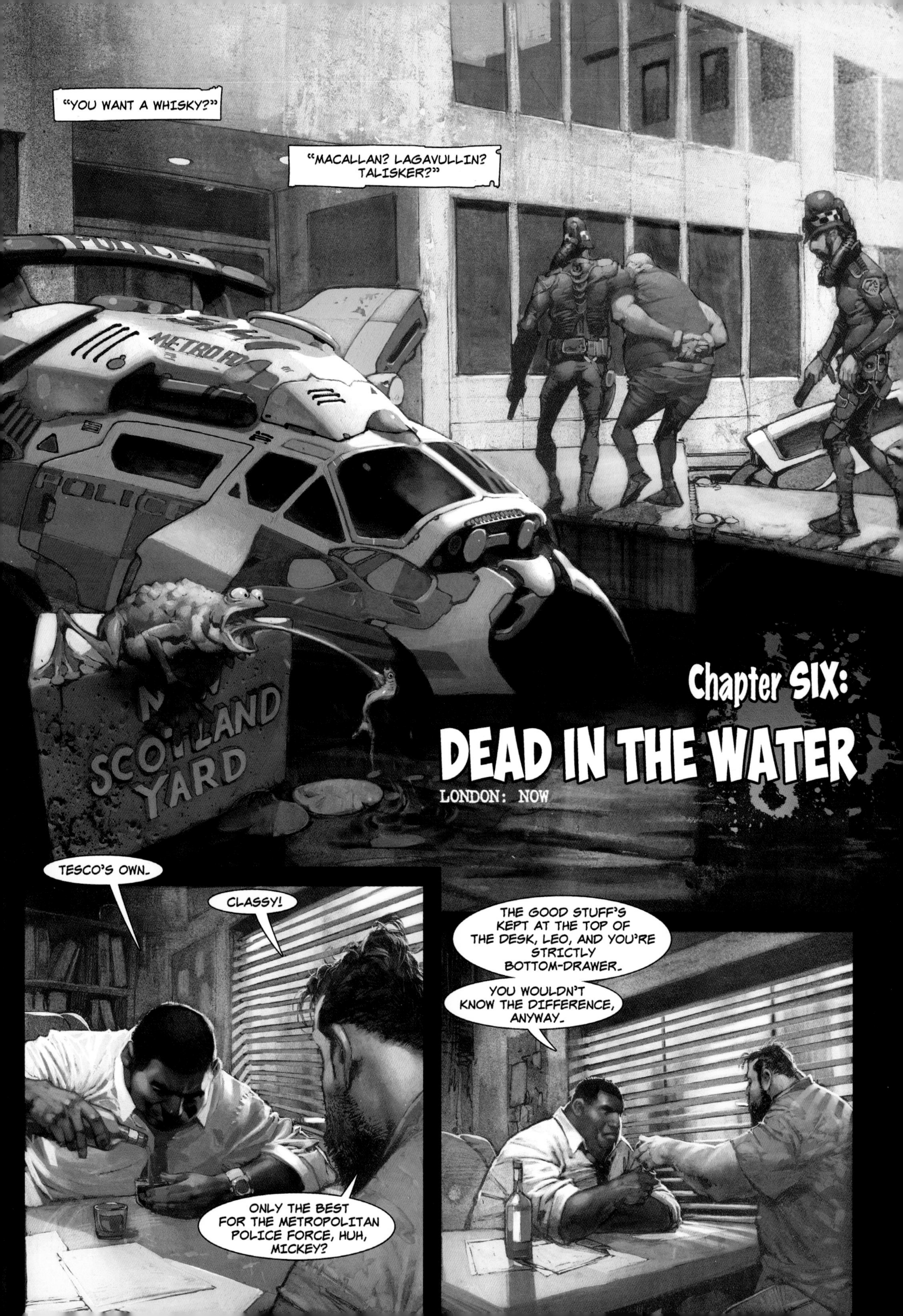
"YOU WANT A WHISKY?"
"MACALLAN? LAGAVULLIN? TALISKER?"
POLICE
METRO
POLICE
NEW SCOTLAND YARD
Chapter SIX:
DEAD IN THE WATER
LONDON: NOW
TESCO'S OWN.
CLASSY!
ONLY THE BEST FOR THE METROPOLITAN POLICE FORCE, HUH, MICKEY?
THE GOOD STUFF'S KEPT AT THE TOP OF THE DESK, LEO, AND YOU'RE STRICTLY BOTTOM-DRAWER.
YOU WOULDN'T KNOW THE DIFFERENCE, ANYWAY.

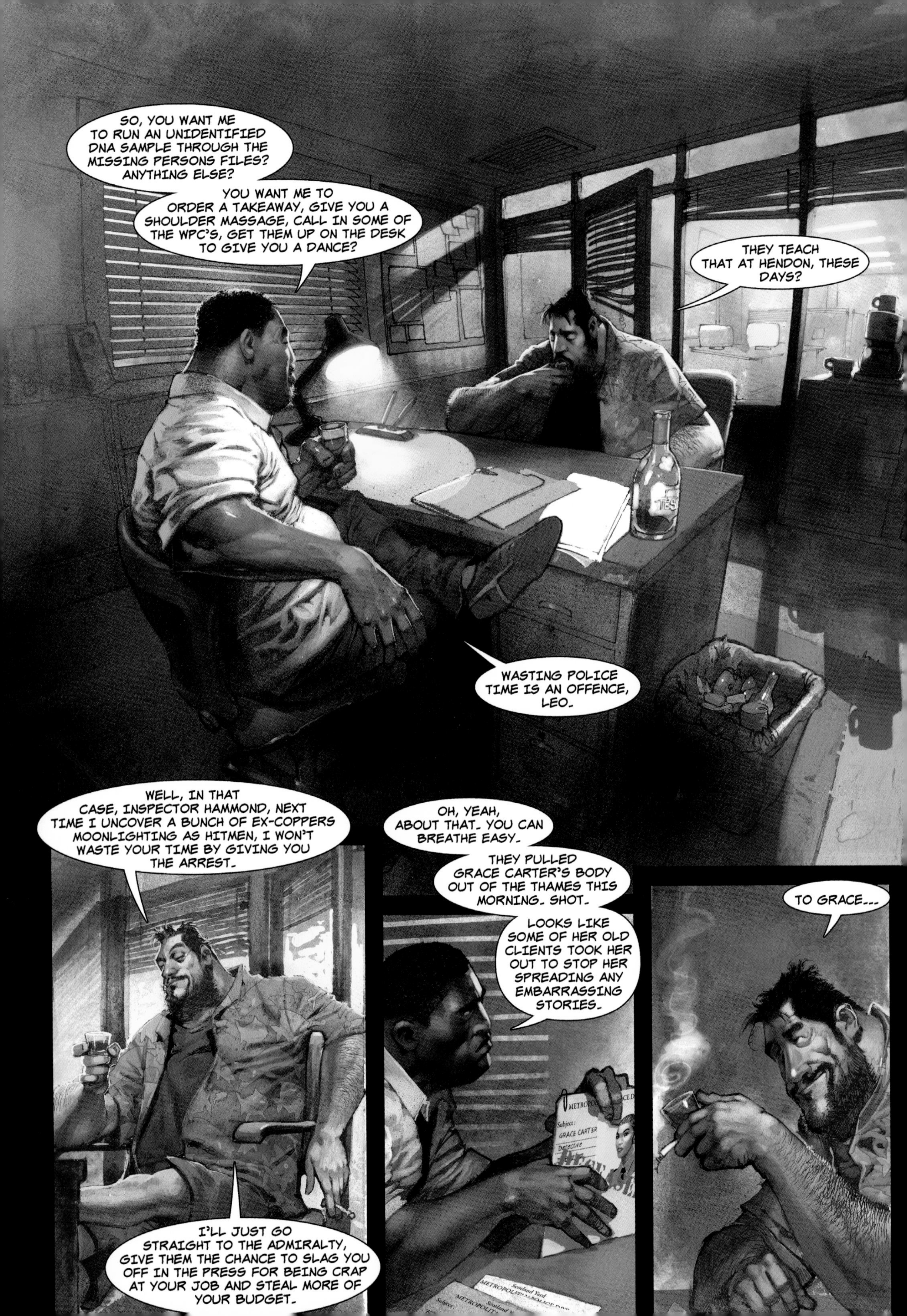
SO, YOU WANT ME TO RUN AN UNIDENTIFIED DNA SAMPLE THROUGH THE MISSING PERSONS FILES? ANYTHING ELSE?
YOU WANT ME TO ORDER A TAKEAWAY, GIVE YOU A SHOULDER MASSAGE, CALL IN SOME OF THE WPC'S, GET THEM UP ON THE DESK TO GIVE YOU A DANCE?
THEY TEACH THAT AT HENDON, THESE DAYS?
WASTING POLICE TIME IS AN OFFENCE, LEO.
WELL, IN THAT CASE, INSPECTOR HAMMOND, NEXT TIME I UNCOVER A BUNCH OF EX-COPPERS MOONLIGHTING AS HITMEN, I WON'T WASTE YOUR TIME BY GIVING YOU THE ARREST.
I'LL JUST GO STRAIGHT TO THE ADMIRALTY, GIVE THEM THE CHANCE TO SLAG YOU OFF IN THE PRESS FOR BEING CRAP AT YOUR JOB AND STEAL MORE OF YOUR BUDGET.
OH, YEAH, ABOUT THAT. YOU CAN BREATHE EASY.
THEY PULLED GRACE CARTER'S BODY OUT OF THE THAMES THIS MORNING. SHOT.
LOOKS LIKE SOME OF HER OLD CLIENTS TOOK HER OUT TO STOP HER SPREADING ANY EMBARRASSING STORIES.
Subject:
GRACE CARTER
TO GRACE...

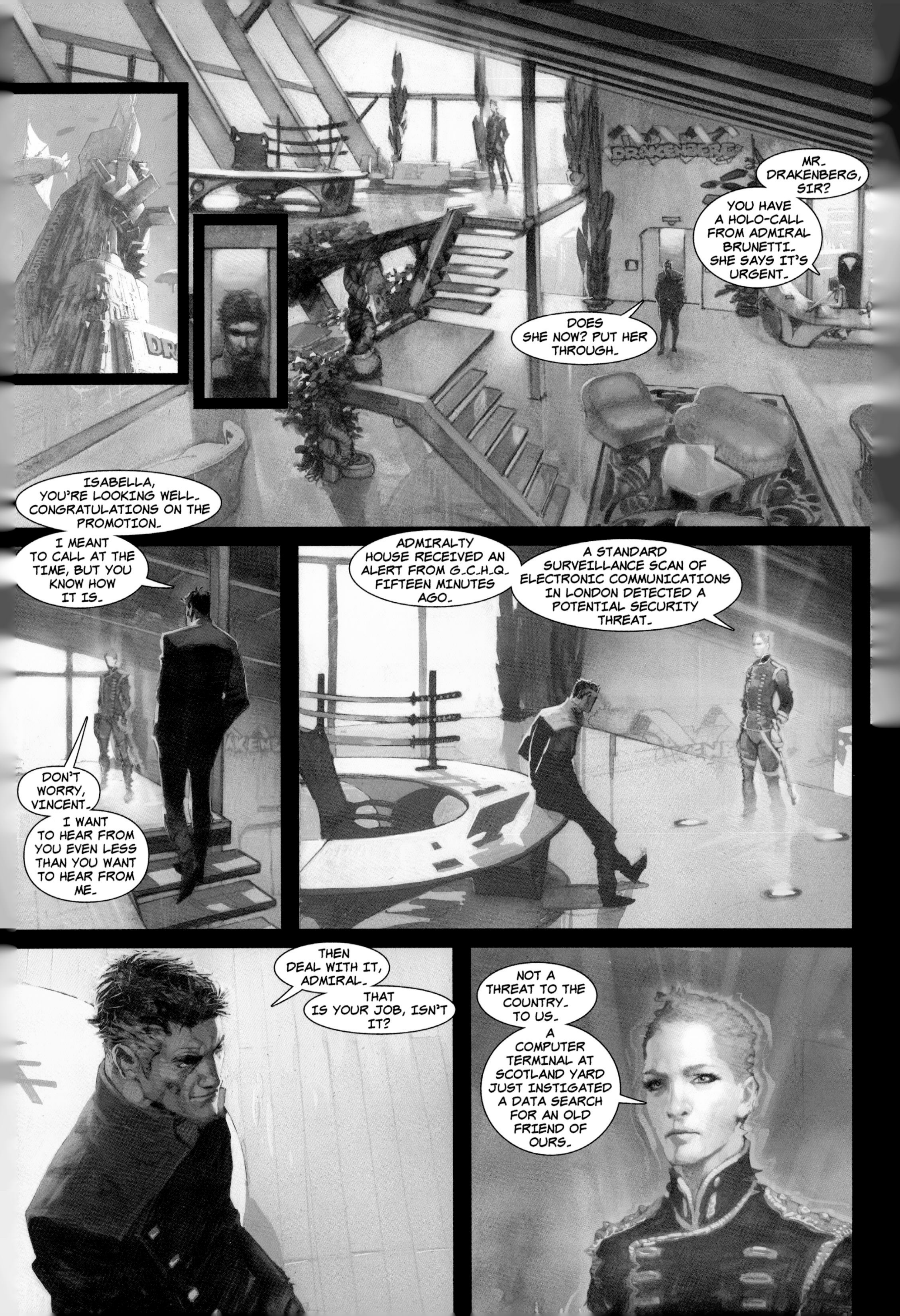

MR. DRAKENBERG, SIR?
YOU HAVE A HOLO-CALL FROM ADMIRAL BRUNETTI. SHE SAYS IT'S URGENT.
DOES SHE NOW? PUT HER THROUGH.
ISABELLA, YOU'RE LOOKING WELL. CONGRATULATIONS ON THE PROMOTION.
I MEANT TO CALL AT THE TIME, BUT YOU KNOW HOW IT IS.
DON'T WORRY, VINCENT.
I WANT TO HEAR FROM YOU EVEN LESS THAN YOU WANT TO HEAR FROM ME.
ADMIRALTY HOUSE RECEIVED AN ALERT FROM G.C.H.Q. FIFTEEN MINUTES AGO.
A STANDARD SURVEILLANCE SCAN OF ELECTRONIC COMMUNICATIONS IN LONDON DETECTED A POTENTIAL SECURITY THREAT.
THEN DEAL WITH IT, ADMIRAL.
THAT IS YOUR JOB, ISN'T IT?
NOT A THREAT TO THE COUNTRY. TO US.
A COMPUTER TERMINAL AT SCOTLAND YARD JUST INSTIGATED A DATA SEARCH FOR AN OLD FRIEND OF OURS.

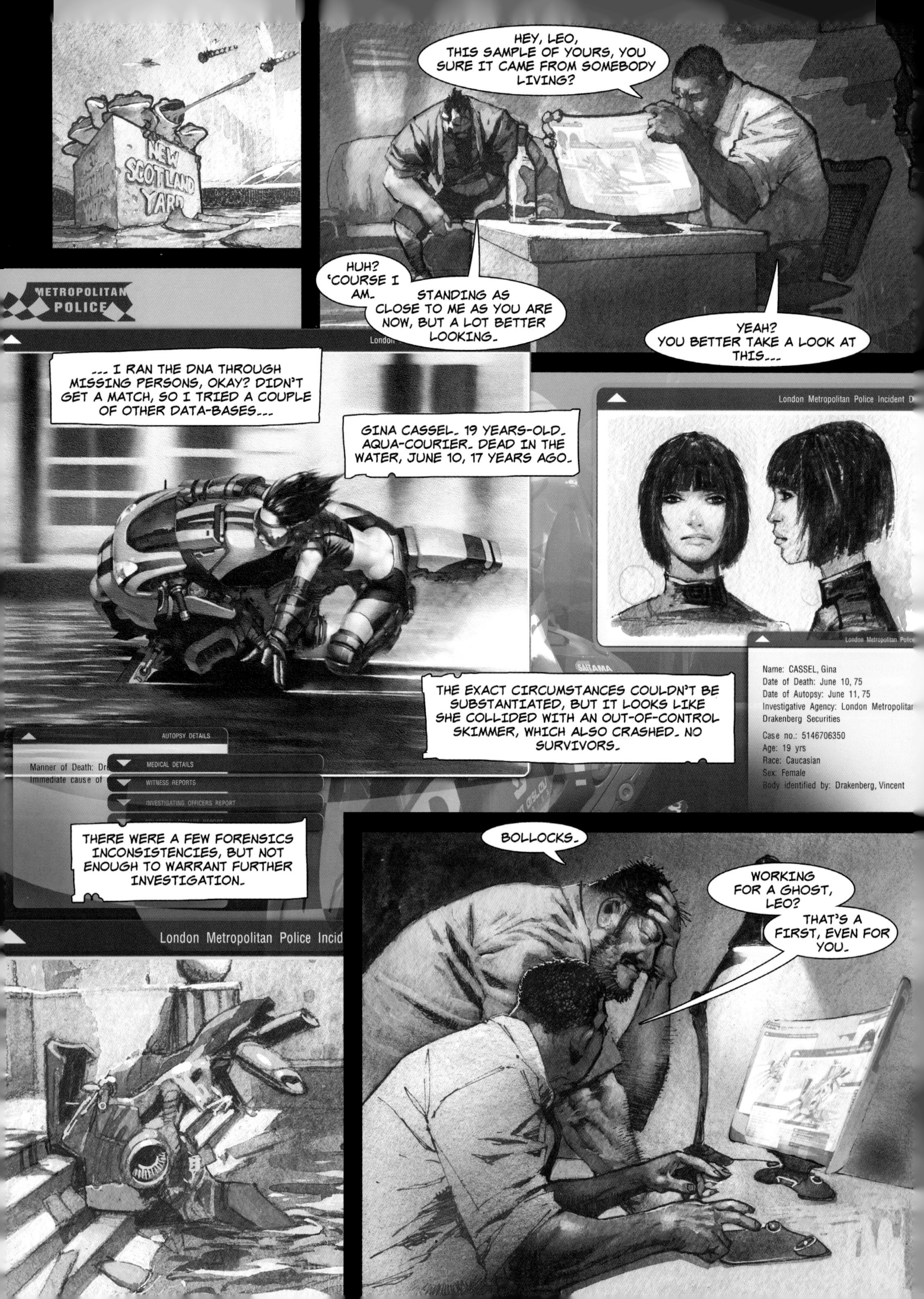

NEW SCOTLAND YARD
HEY, LEO, THIS SAMPLE OF YOURS, YOU SURE IT CAME FROM SOMEBODY LIVING?
HUH? 'COURSE I AM.
STANDING AS CLOSE TO ME AS YOU ARE NOW, BUT A LOT BETTER LOOKING.
YEAH? YOU BETTER TAKE A LOOK AT THIS...
METROPOLITAN POLICE
... I RAN THE DNA THROUGH MISSING PERSONS, OKAY? DIDN'T GET A MATCH, SO I TRIED A COUPLE OF OTHER DATA-BASES...
GINA CASSEL. 19 YEARS-OLD. AQUA-COURIER. DEAD IN THE WATER, JUNE 10, 17 YEARS AGO.
London Metropolitan Police Incident D
London Metropolitan Police
Name: CASSEL, Gina
Date of Death: June 10, 75
Date of Autopsy: June 11, 75
Investigative Agency: London Metropolitan
Drakenberg Securities
Case no.: 5146706350
Age: 19 yrs
Race: Caucasian
Sex: Female
Body identified by: Drakenberg, Vincent
SAITAMA
THE EXACT CIRCUMSTANCES COULDN'T BE SUBSTANTIATED, BUT IT LOOKS LIKE SHE COLLIDED WITH AN OUT-OF-CONTROL SKIMMER, WHICH ALSO CRASHED. NO SURVIVORS.
AUTOPSY DETAILS
Manner of Death:
Immediate cause of
MEDICAL DETAILS
WITNESS REPORTS
INVESTIGATING OFFICERS REPORT
THERE WERE A FEW FORENSICS INCONSISTENCIES, BUT NOT ENOUGH TO WARRANT FURTHER INVESTIGATION.
London Metropolitan Police Incid
BOLLOCKS.
WORKING FOR A GHOST, LEO?
THAT'S A FIRST, EVEN FOR YOU.

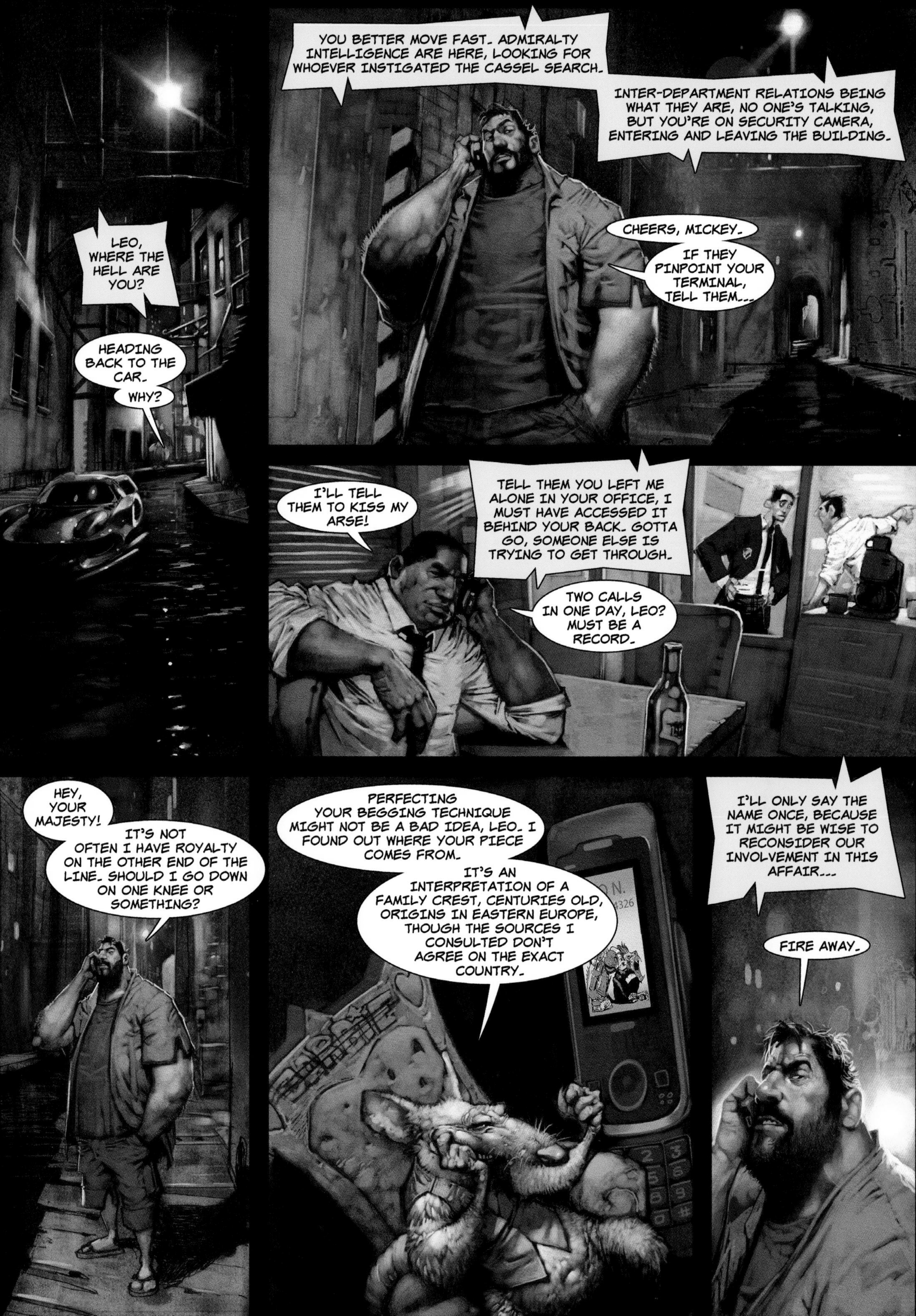
LEO, WHERE THE HELL ARE YOU?
HEADING BACK TO THE CAR.
WHY?
YOU BETTER MOVE FAST. ADMIRALTY INTELLIGENCE ARE HERE, LOOKING FOR WHOEVER INSTIGATED THE CASSEL SEARCH.
INTER-DEPARTMENT RELATIONS BEING WHAT THEY ARE, NO ONE'S TALKING, BUT YOU'RE ON SECURITY CAMERA, ENTERING AND LEAVING THE BUILDING.
CHEERS, MICKEY.
IF THEY PINPOINT YOUR TERMINAL, TELL THEM...
I'LL TELL THEM TO KISS MY ARSE!
TELL THEM YOU LEFT ME ALONE IN YOUR OFFICE, I MUST HAVE ACCESSED IT BEHIND YOUR BACK. GOTTA GO, SOMEONE ELSE IS TRYING TO GET THROUGH.
TWO CALLS IN ONE DAY, LEO? MUST BE A RECORD.
HEY, YOUR MAJESTY!
IT'S NOT OFTEN I HAVE ROYALTY ON THE OTHER END OF THE LINE. SHOULD I GO DOWN ON ONE KNEE OR SOMETHING?
PERFECTING YOUR BEGGING TECHNIQUE MIGHT NOT BE A BAD IDEA, LEO. I FOUND OUT WHERE YOUR PIECE COMES FROM.
IT'S AN INTERPRETATION OF A FAMILY CREST, CENTURIES OLD, ORIGINS IN EASTERN EUROPE, THOUGH THE SOURCES I CONSULTED DON'T AGREE ON THE EXACT COUNTRY.
I'LL ONLY SAY THE NAME ONCE, BECAUSE IT MIGHT BE WISE TO RECONSIDER OUR INVOLVEMENT IN THIS AFFAIR...
FIRE AWAY.

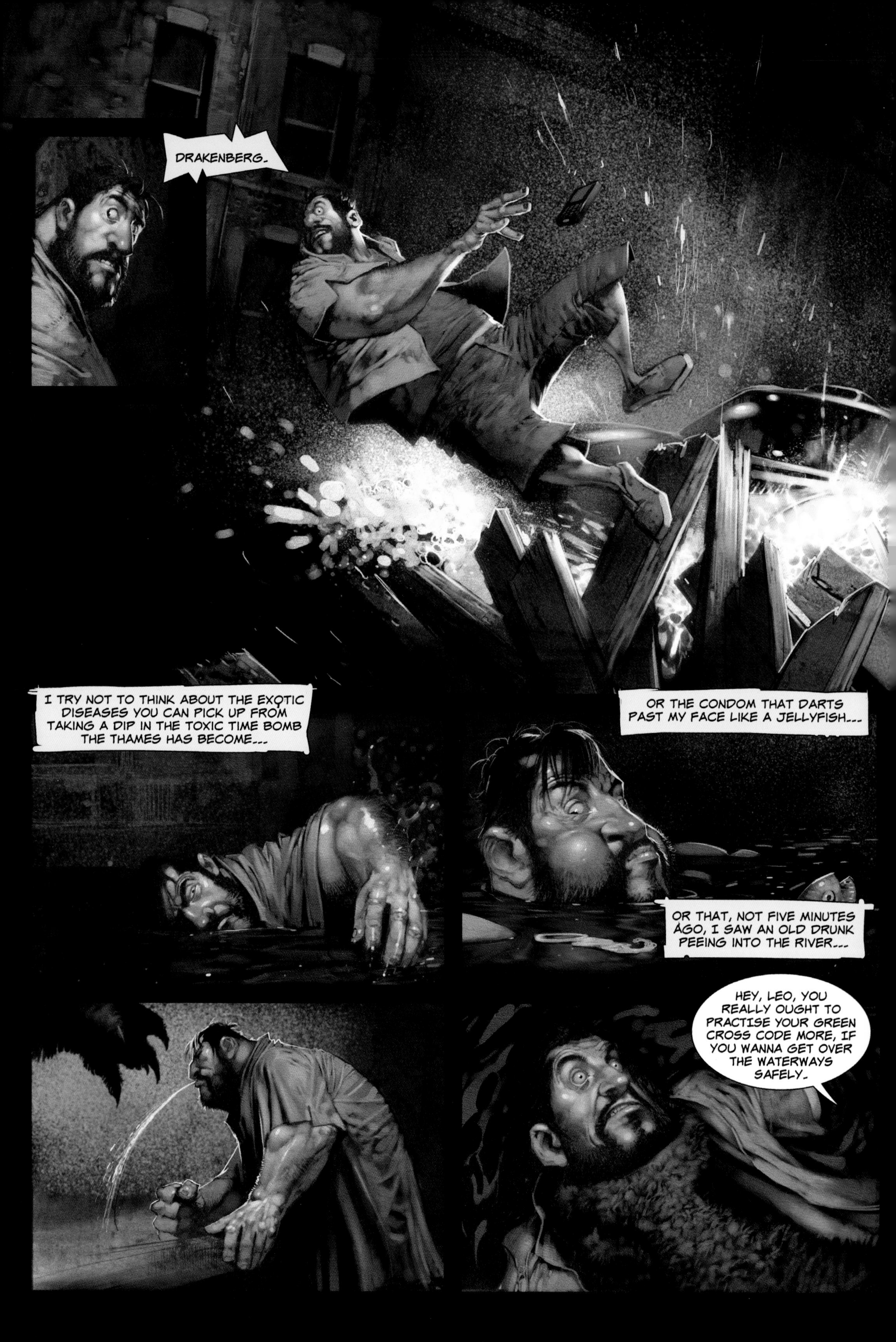
DRAKENBERG.
I TRY NOT TO THINK ABOUT THE EXOTIC DISEASES YOU CAN PICK UP FROM TAKING A DIP IN THE TOXIC TIME BOMB THE THAMES HAS BECOME...
OR THE CONDOM THAT DARTS PAST MY FACE LIKE A JELLYFISH...
OR THAT, NOT FIVE MINUTES AGO, I SAW AN OLD DRUNK PEEING INTO THE RIVER...
HEY, LEO, YOU REALLY OUGHT TO PRACTISE YOUR GREEN CROSS CODE MORE, IF YOU WANNA GET OVER THE WATERWAYS SAFELY.

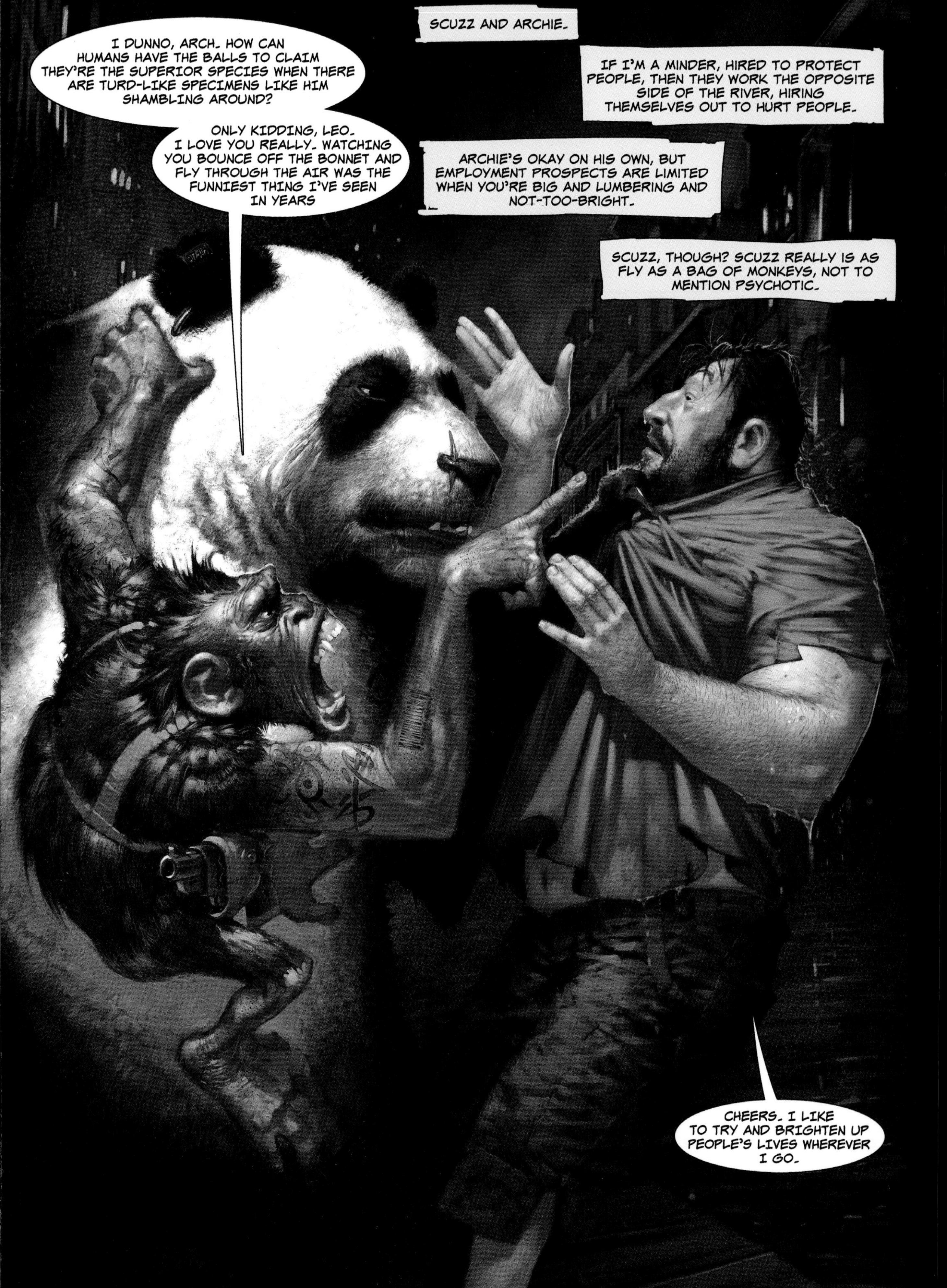
SCUZZ AND ARCHIE.
I DUNNO, ARCH. HOW CAN HUMANS HAVE THE BALLS TO CLAIM THEY'RE THE SUPERIOR SPECIES WHEN THERE ARE TURD-LIKE SPECIMENS LIKE HIM SHAMBLING AROUND?
IF I'M A MINDER, HIRED TO PROTECT PEOPLE, THEN THEY WORK THE OPPOSITE SIDE OF THE RIVER, HIRING THEMSELVES OUT TO HURT PEOPLE.
ONLY KIDDING, LEO. I LOVE YOU REALLY. WATCHING YOU BOUNCE OFF THE BONNET AND FLY THROUGH THE AIR WAS THE FUNNIEST THING I'VE SEEN IN YEARS
ARCHIE'S OKAY ON HIS OWN, BUT EMPLOYMENT PROSPECTS ARE LIMITED WHEN YOU'RE BIG AND LUMBERING AND NOT-TOO-BRIGHT.
SCUZZ, THOUGH? SCUZZ REALLY IS AS FLY AS A BAG OF MONKEYS, NOT TO MENTION PSYCHOTIC.
CHEERS. I LIKE TO TRY AND BRIGHTEN UP PEOPLE'S LIVES WHEREVER I GO.

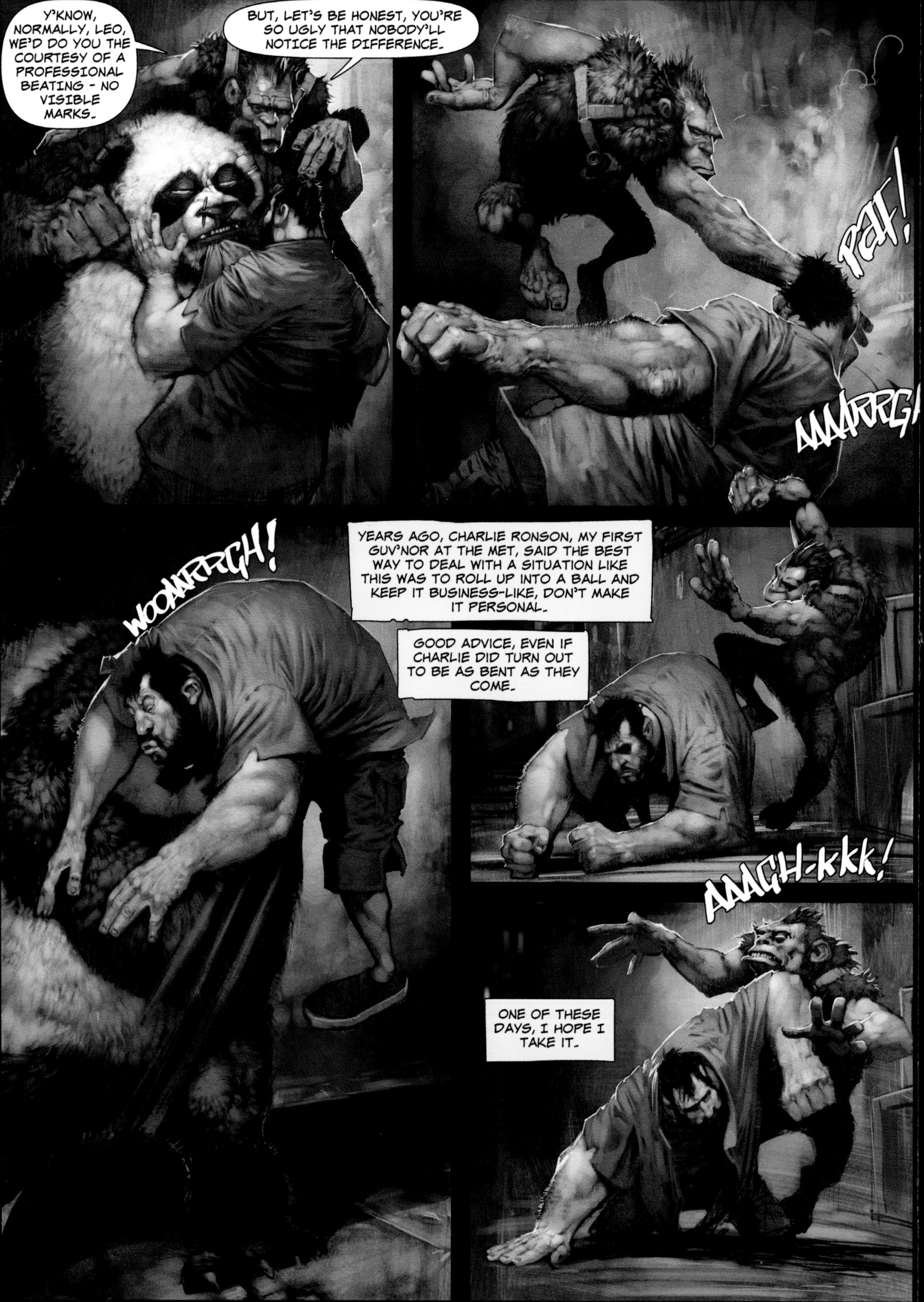
Y'KNOW, NORMALLY, LEO, WE'D DO YOU THE COURTESY OF A PROFESSIONAL BEATING - NO VISIBLE MARKS.
BUT, LET'S BE HONEST, YOU'RE SO UGLY THAT NOBODY'LL NOTICE THE DIFFERENCE.
PAF!
AAAARRG!
WOOAARRGH!
YEARS AGO, CHARLIE RONSON, MY FIRST GUV'NOR AT THE MET, SAID THE BEST WAY TO DEAL WITH A SITUATION LIKE THIS WAS TO ROLL UP INTO A BALL AND KEEP IT BUSINESS-LIKE, DON'T MAKE IT PERSONAL.
GOOD ADVICE, EVEN IF CHARLIE DID TURN OUT TO BE AS BENT AS THEY COME.
AAAGH-KKK!
ONE OF THESE DAYS, I HOPE I TAKE IT.

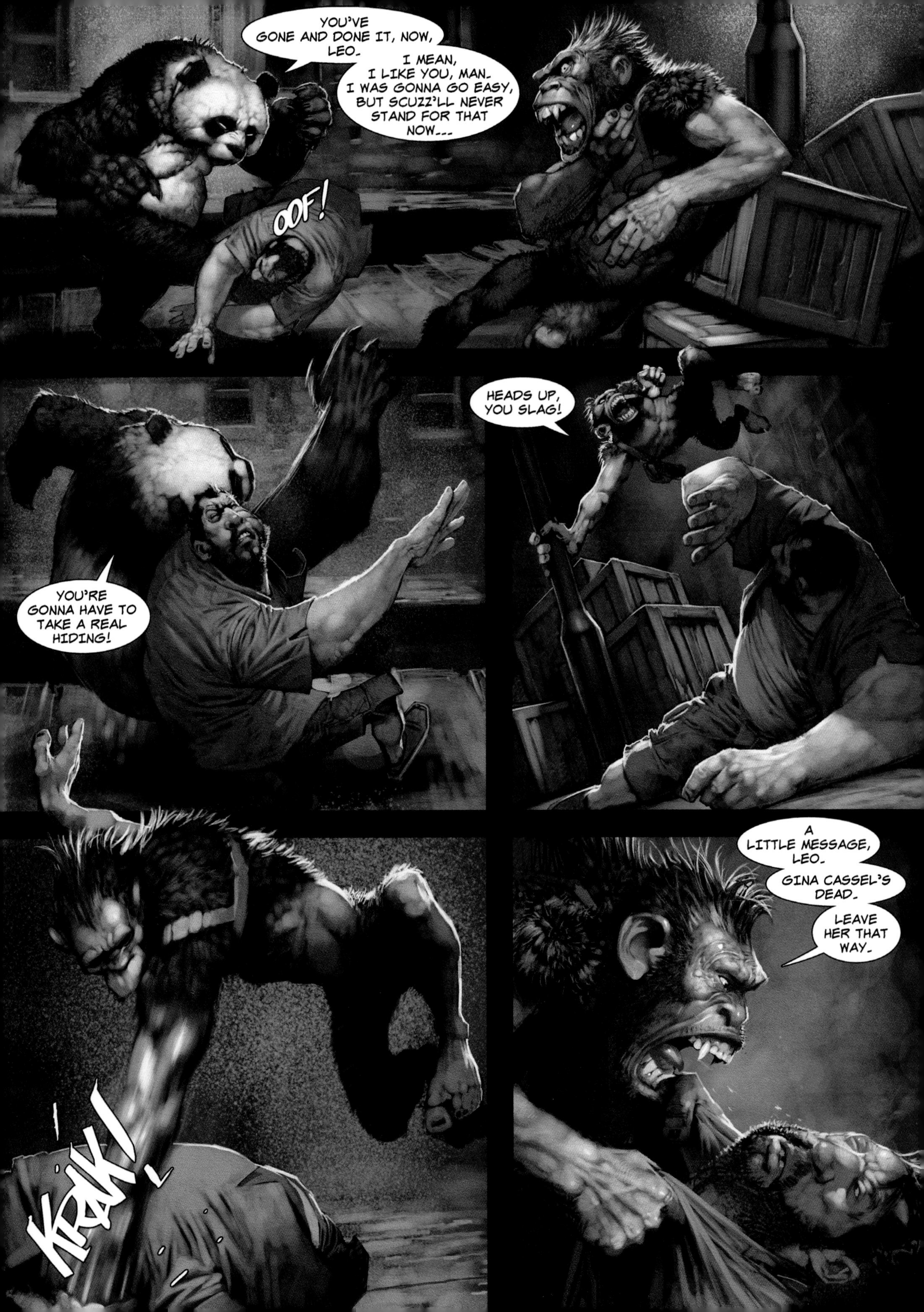

YOU'VE GONE AND DONE IT, NOW, LEO.
I MEAN, I LIKE YOU, MAN. I WAS GONNA GO EASY, BUT SCUZZ'LL NEVER STAND FOR THAT NOW...
OOF!
YOU'RE GONNA HAVE TO TAKE A REAL HIDING!
HEADS UP, YOU SLAG!
KRAK!
A LITTLE MESSAGE, LEO.
GINA CASSEL'S DEAD.
LEAVE HER THAT WAY.

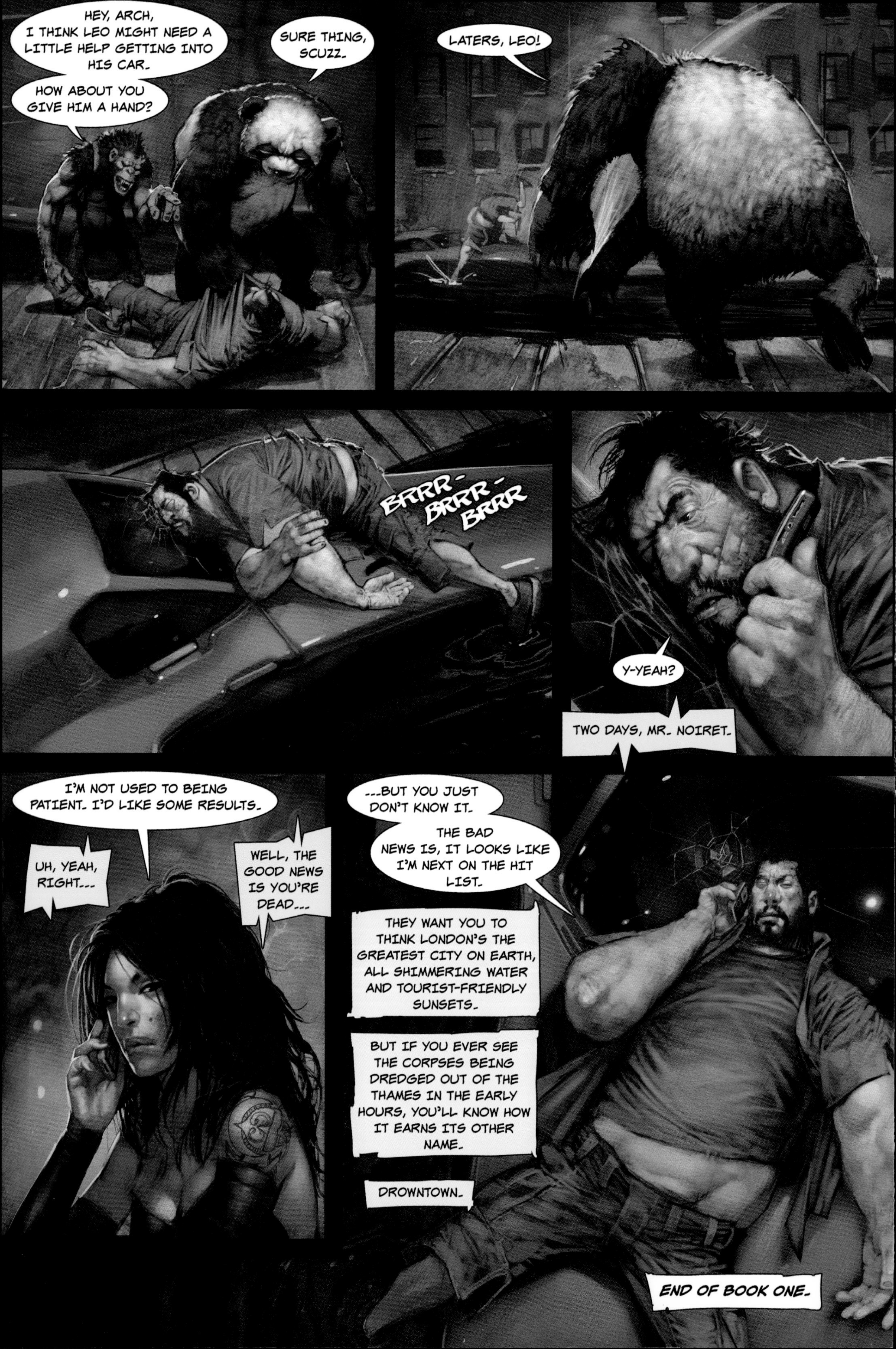

HEY, ARCH, I THINK LEO MIGHT NEED A LITTLE HELP GETTING INTO HIS CAR.
HOW ABOUT YOU GIVE HIM A HAND?
SURE THING, SCUZZ.
LATERS, LEO!
BRRR-BRRR-BRRR
Y-YEAH?
TWO DAYS, MR. NOIRET.
I'M NOT USED TO BEING PATIENT. I'D LIKE SOME RESULTS.
UH, YEAH, RIGHT...
WELL, THE GOOD NEWS IS YOU'RE DEAD...
...BUT YOU JUST DON'T KNOW IT.
THE BAD NEWS IS, IT LOOKS LIKE I'M NEXT ON THE HIT LIST.
THEY WANT YOU TO THINK LONDON'S THE GREATEST CITY ON EARTH, ALL SHIMMERING WATER AND TOURIST-FRIENDLY SUNSETS.
BUT IF YOU EVER SEE THE CORPSES BEING DREDGED OUT OF THE THAMES IN THE EARLY HOURS, YOU'LL KNOW HOW IT EARNS ITS OTHER NAME.
DROWNTOWN.
END OF BOOK ONE.

Other graphic novels by Robbie Morrison include:

**White Death**
(Artist: Charlie Adlard)

**The Adventures of Nikolai Dante**
(Artists: Simon Fraser, John Burns and others

Book 1: The Romanov Dynasty
Book 2: The Great Game
Book 3: The Courtship of Jena Makarov
Book 4: Tsar Wars Vol. 1
Book 5: Tsar Wars Vol. 2
Book 6: Hell and High Water
Book 7: The Sword of the Tsar
Book 8: The Beast of Rudunshtein
Book 9: Amerika
Book 10: Hero of the Revolution
Book 11: Sympathy for the Devil

**Shakara**
(Artist: Henry Flint)

Book 1: Avenger
Book 2: Destroyer

Other books by Jim Murray

**Batman: Judge Dredd (Die Laughing)**

**Batman & Demon: A Tragedy**

**Dota 2: Tales from the Secret Shop**
(http://www.dota2.com/comics/are_we_heroes_yet/)

Published by Jonathan Cape 2013

2 4 6 8 10 9 7 5 3 1



First published in Great Britain in 2013 by
Jonathan Cape
Random House, 20 Vauxhall Bridge Road,
London SW1V 2SA

www.vintage-books.co.uk

Addresses for companies within The Random House Group Limited can be found at:
www.randomhouse.co.uk/offices.htm

The Random House Group Limited Reg. No. 954009

A CIP catalogue record for this book is available from the British Library

ISBN 9780224085878

The Random House Group Limited supports the Forest Stewardship Council ®(FSC ®), the leading international forest-certification organisation. Our books carrying the FSC label are printed on FSC® -certified paper. FSC is the only forest-certification scheme supported by the leading environmental organisations, including Greenpeace. Our paper procurement policy can be found at www.randomhouse.co.uk/environment

MIX
Paper from responsible sources
FSC® C008047

Printed and bound in China by C&C Offset Printing Co., Ltd

T 101507

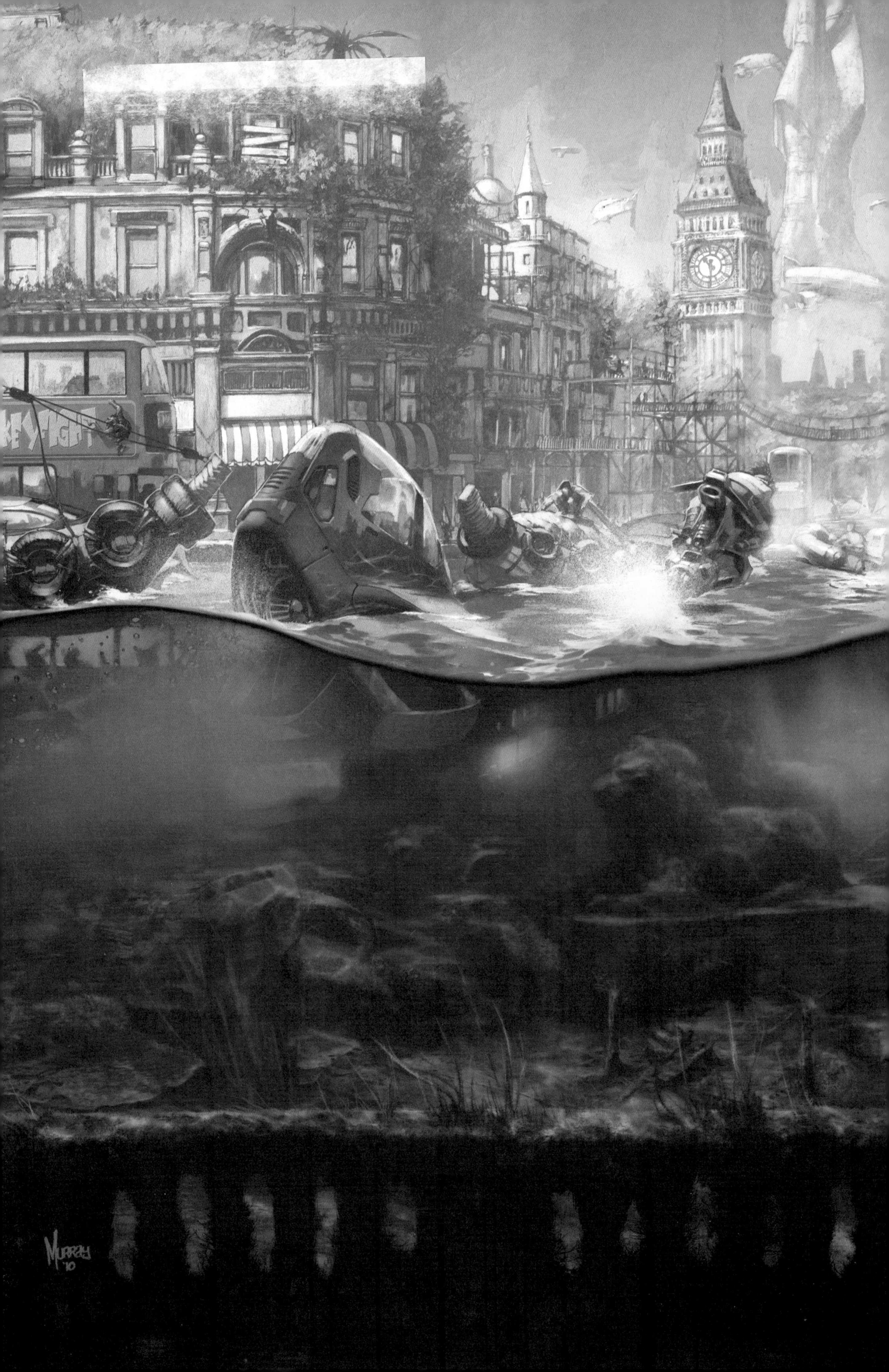
MURRAY
'10